# The Drummer's Studio Survival Guide

## How to get the best possible drum tracks on any recording project

by **Mark Huntly Parsons**

Edited by **Rick Van Horn**

**Design and Layout**
**Javier Jimenez**

Published by:
Modern Drummer Publications, Inc.
12 Old Bridge Road
Cedar Grove, New Jersey 07009 U.S.A.

# Table Of Contents

FOR WENDELIN
My partner, best friend, wife, and catalyst of my aspirations...
You're the best!

# Acknowledgements

**Kenny Aronoff**

**Ross Garfield**

**Bob Gatzen**

**Jim Keltner**

**Rod Morgenstein**

**Simon Phillips**

**John "J.R." Robinson**

**Ed Thacker**

First of all, a huge thank you to Ron Spagnardi, Rick Van Horn, and the rest of the folks at Modern Drummer Publications, without whom you wouldn't be holding this book in your hands. Before anything becomes a reality, it's first a dream. These guys have been instrumental in helping to make this particular dream come true, from giving me a shot at writing for *MD*, to providing the original impetus for the "Studio Survival Guide" series, to enthusiastically agreeing to the idea of expanding that series into a book—all the while keeping me on the path with expert editorial guidance. Muchas gracias, amigos!

Special thanks to Gregg Bissonette (who took the time from his busy schedule to read the manuscript and write the foreword), and to the rest of our "panel of pros" who also gave generously of their time and insight: Kenny Aronoff, Mike Fraser, Ross Garfield, Bob Gatzen, Jim Keltner, Rod Morgenstein, Simon Phillips, J.R. Robinson, and Ed Thacker.

Loving thanks to Ed, Rosalyn, Les, and Eric (who've always been supportive of my creative efforts), to John Pillow (resolute stalwart of the first order), and to Bracky (oops...I mean *Bill*) Simpson (with whom I made my first forays into the magic worlds of music and recording).

And finally, the completion of this manuscript is dedicated to the recently departed Chuck Hensley, fellow member of the Diablo Canyon Writers' Support Group. Thanks, Coach!

Selected photographs courtesy of the following companies: AKG, Alesis, Aphex, ART, Ashley, Audio-Technica, Audix, beyerdynamic, Cave Studio, dbx, Digitech, Electro-Voice, Eventide, JBL, K&K Sound Systems, Lexicon, Mackie, Marantz, Moon Recording, Neumann, Ocean Way Studio, Otari, Panasonic, Rane, Polar Productions, Sennheiser, Shure, Sony, Tascam, and Yamaha.

# Foreword

Lissa Wales

Every time I listen to my favorite band, the Beatles, I either consciously or unconsciously thank their producer (George Martin) and their various engineers (Geoff Emerick, Norman Smith, Ken Scott, and others) for capturing such wonderful performances on tape so well. During the recording process they carefully balanced the levels in a very magical way. Had it not been for their recording expertise, musical history wouldn't be the same. Neither would the drum tracks of Ringo Starr.

In *The Drummer's Studio Survival Guide*, Mark Parsons brilliantly bridges the gap between producer, engineer, and drummer. Mark is right when he states that "communication is the key." Just like in any relationship, you've got to communicate about what you want and need. From attitude to microphone selection, from tuning, drum equipment, and muffling to room sounds, physics, and mic' placement, and from compressors, limiters, noise gates, and digital effects to recording consoles, pre-production, mixing, and many other topics, this book gets you up to date on what you need to know in order to make that communication happen. (I found the glossary of terms especially helpful!) Additionally, the "Ask The Pros" sections pose lots of pertinent questions with lots of great and varied answers.

Thanks, Mark, for a much-needed book that fills the void extremely well.

**Gregg Bissonette**

# Introduction

## Why Bother?

The purpose of this book is to help you improve your recorded drum sound, and although it's primarily aimed at drummers, it will also benefit those on the other side of the glass. Why bother learning about recording drums? If you're a drummer, shouldn't you just rely on the engineer, and shouldn't the engineer already know all this stuff?

Good questions. Yes, most professional engineers working at major studios are very good at what they do. But due to recent advancements in recording technology there's been a huge influx of home and "project" studios. For many of the folks working in these smaller facilities, the primary drum recording experience has consisted of plugging a sequencer into a drum module or taking a line out of a MIDI drumset and going to tape with it. This is fine for songwriting demos and other incidental recordings, but it's a far cry from the challenging task of capturing real, live drums on tape. The information presented here will give those folks a leg up on the process—not just from a technical viewpoint (though there's plenty of that), but also with an eye towards what goes into the making of a good drum track, including the equipment, the recording environment, and the attitude of everyone involved.

Now, what about *drummers* needing to know this stuff? Well, if you as a drummer are going to be recording, you'll probably find yourself in one of the three following situations, and you'll profit from a knowledge of recording techniques in each one of them.

First, there's a good chance you'll end up in the scenario described above—where you're recording in a project studio and the engineer may not have years of experience recording real drums. And while that engineer probably knows how to operate *his* (or *her*) equipment very well, it's obvious that in this situation any practical tips you can offer on how to record *your* drums will benefit the process.

Then again, you may be fortunate enough to find yourself in a large commercial studio. In this case, assuming that the engineer's skills are commensurate with the quality of the studio, you certainly won't have to tell him what sort of microphone to use on your kick drum. He's sure to be a professional who knows what he's doing. But by the same token, *you're* the one most familiar with how your drums should sound. It would be good for you to know at least enough to be able to accurately convey your feelings about the matter, if appropriate. That way, instead of merely complaining that he made your snare sound like paper, you could request to hear the track again with (for example) a three dB boost at 200 Hz on the snare. (We'll also discuss the politics of these sorts of suggestions, including times when they're *not* appropriate.) And even if you happen to absolutely *love* the drum sound the engineer's getting, it sure would be great if you understood enough about the technical side of things to pick up some pointers from him for future use.

There's a third option that's becoming more and more popular as high-quality recording equipment gets increasingly more affordable: You or one of your bandmembers may own one or more modular digital multitracks, and you might decide to produce your own tape. In this case the sound of your drum tracks will be *totally* up to you, and you're going to want every bit of information you can get—from here and elsewhere. You're still going to have to do a lot of hands-on experimentation, but this book can serve as a road map and keep you from getting lost in the weeds. (And believe me, there are a *lot* of weeds out there.)

Regular readers of *Modern Drummer* magazine will recognize that this book is based on the "Studio Survival Guide" series that was published therein between April of 1995 and April of 1996. However, the contents have been reworked and updated (a "Second Edition," if you will) by the addition of some new material and graphics to help clarify things. Also, things have been arranged as much as possible to parallel the order of events a drummer would follow if he or she were going through the recording process from start to finish.

During the course of writing this book I interviewed several professional drummers and a couple of pro engineers. At the end of certain chapters their views on the subject at hand are presented in a section called "Ask The Pros." The drummers on our panel of experts include Kenny Aronoff, Gregg Bissonette, Jim Keltner, Rod Morgenstein, Simon Phillips, and John "J.R." Robinson. Each of these drummers is a household name in the music industry, and each has proven himself to be extremely musical in a wide variety of situations. Yet each has a style and vision that is uniquely his own.

For the section on drum prep I also solicited input from two other experts: Ross Garfield and Bob Gatzen. Ross (better known as "The Drum Doctor") is probably the most renowned drum technician working today. As for Bob...well, for Bob the best description is probably: D) All of the above. He's a drummer, an engineer, a producer, and a drum designer, so he views the situation from all sides.

Supplying the perspective from the other side of the glass are recording engineers Ed Thacker and Mike Fraser. Ed has worked with a number of top acts, including 10,000 Maniacs, XTC, Bruce Hornsby, Heart, and Sass Jordan. Mike lists among his credits such rock icons as Aerosmith, AC/DC, the Cult, Coverdale-Page, and Blue Murder.

All of these gentlemen are the cream of the crop. They work at a world-class level—and they do it every day for a living. Obviously their advice should be given serious consideration. However, an interesting note arises: You'll notice that they don't always agree on the best way to do things. This doesn't mean that some are right and some are wrong. Quite the contrary. They're *all* correct, because the subject of recording drums isn't just cold, hard science. It's art, it's craft, it's technique, it's talent, it's magic. In short, it's *music*. Enjoy.

# CHAPTER 1

# Everything Counts (An Overview)

Which aspects of the process *really* matter when you're recording your drums, and which can be safely ignored? As you've probably guessed from the title of this chapter, everything will affect the sound to one degree or another, and we owe it to ourselves to try to optimize every variable within our control (and budget!).

Here's why we can't ignore the small stuff: *Errors are cumulative*—even ones too small to actually hear by themselves. Imagine that you have two very high-quality cassette decks, and you use one of them to make a dub of a master tape being played in the other deck. Assuming you do everything just right (best tape, best noise reduction scheme, etc.), it's possible that you could produce a dub that sounded "just like" the original. (They aren't really identical, of course, it's just that the differences may not be audible.)

Now take that dub and make a copy of it, then make a copy of *that* copy, and so on, with each one supposedly sounding just like the last. In short order you'll find a distressing difference between the original tape and one a few generations removed—leading to the inescapable conclusion that *inaudible* errors add up to very *audible* results. If this is true, imagine what happens when *obvious* degradations are allowed to remain in the chain.

This situation applies to artistic matters as well

to acoustic ones. For example, let's say that you played a part that was "okay," but not really in the pocket. But you let it slide because "it's only a demo." On top of that, your drumheads were old and a little pitted, and you hadn't tuned your kit in a while. Now suppose the room is a converted square garage with sheetrock on all four walls and a harsh sound—which we could live with, except for the fact that the mic's have been placed too far from the drums so lots of the ugly room sound is leaking in. Then the engineer decides to use dynamic vocal mic's on your cymbals and makes up for their truncated high-end response by adding lots of EQ at 12 kHz. Additionally, you play your cymbals much harder than the rest of your kit, causing them to splatter all over the track. During mixdown you attempt to hide the deficiencies with signal processing—gating the kick and snare to the point where the softer notes disappear, then drowning what's left in a wash of digital reverb. Finally, you make a copy of the finished song on a 99¢ cassette tape.

*Whew.* Are you going to be happy with the results? Although musical taste is largely a matter of opinion, I feel safe in saying that this would not be a recording you'd want to play for your friends. So where did things go wrong? Let's start by looking at the flow chart—titled "Things That Affect Your Drum Sound"—that follows on the next two pages.

# THINGS THAT AFFECT

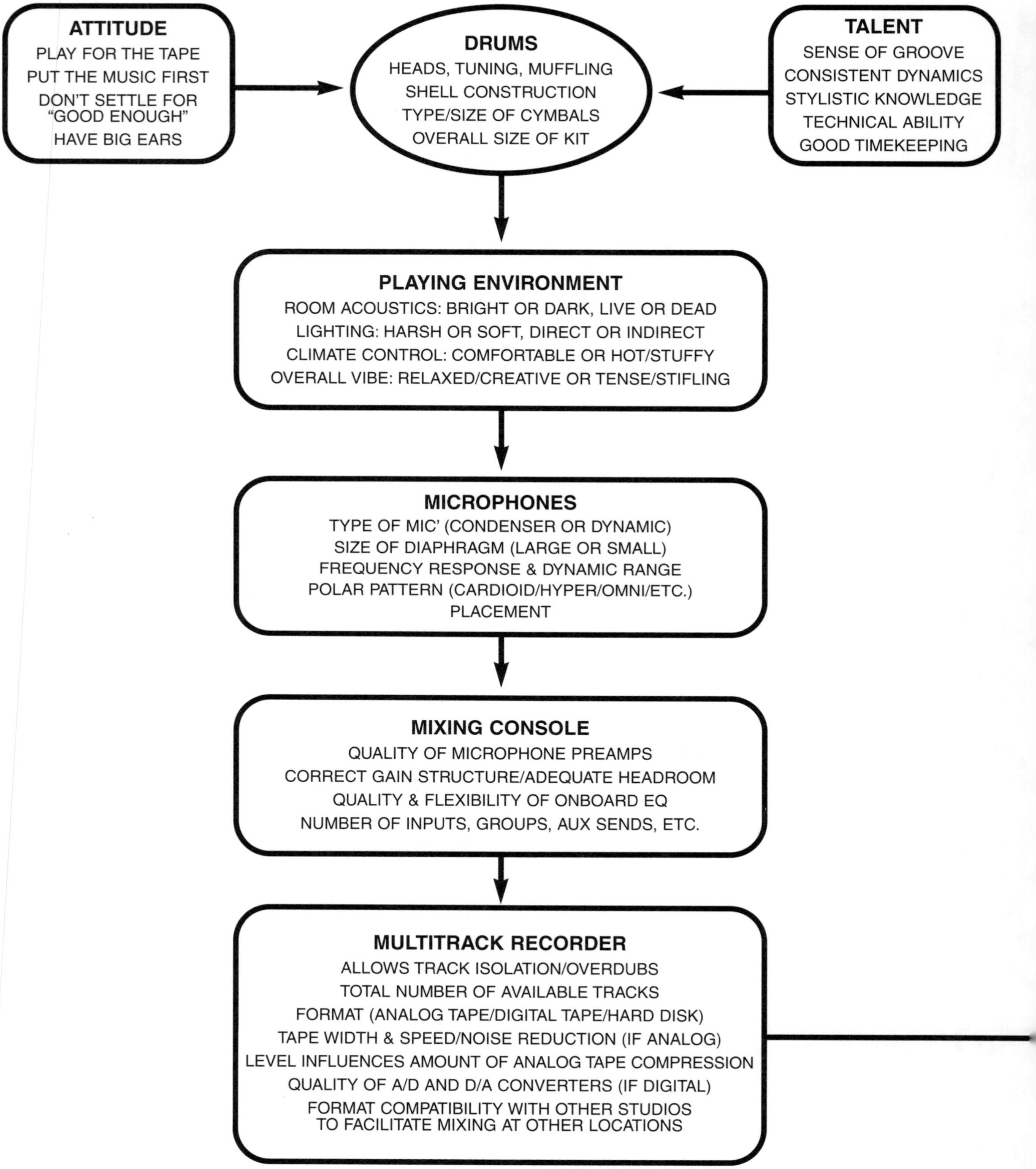

**ATTITUDE**
PLAY FOR THE TAPE
PUT THE MUSIC FIRST
DON'T SETTLE FOR
"GOOD ENOUGH"
HAVE BIG EARS

**DRUMS**
HEADS, TUNING, MUFFLING
SHELL CONSTRUCTION
TYPE/SIZE OF CYMBALS
OVERALL SIZE OF KIT

**TALENT**
SENSE OF GROOVE
CONSISTENT DYNAMICS
STYLISTIC KNOWLEDGE
TECHNICAL ABILITY
GOOD TIMEKEEPING

**PLAYING ENVIRONMENT**
ROOM ACOUSTICS: BRIGHT OR DARK, LIVE OR DEAD
LIGHTING: HARSH OR SOFT, DIRECT OR INDIRECT
CLIMATE CONTROL: COMFORTABLE OR HOT/STUFFY
OVERALL VIBE: RELAXED/CREATIVE OR TENSE/STIFLING

**MICROPHONES**
TYPE OF MIC' (CONDENSER OR DYNAMIC)
SIZE OF DIAPHRAGM (LARGE OR SMALL)
FREQUENCY RESPONSE & DYNAMIC RANGE
POLAR PATTERN (CARDIOID/HYPER/OMNI/ETC.)
PLACEMENT

**MIXING CONSOLE**
QUALITY OF MICROPHONE PREAMPS
CORRECT GAIN STRUCTURE/ADEQUATE HEADROOM
QUALITY & FLEXIBILITY OF ONBOARD EQ
NUMBER OF INPUTS, GROUPS, AUX SENDS, ETC.

**MULTITRACK RECORDER**
ALLOWS TRACK ISOLATION/OVERDUBS
TOTAL NUMBER OF AVAILABLE TRACKS
FORMAT (ANALOG TAPE/DIGITAL TAPE/HARD DISK)
TAPE WIDTH & SPEED/NOISE REDUCTION (IF ANALOG)
LEVEL INFLUENCES AMOUNT OF ANALOG TAPE COMPRESSION
QUALITY OF A/D AND D/A CONVERTERS (IF DIGITAL)
FORMAT COMPATIBILITY WITH OTHER STUDIOS
TO FACILITATE MIXING AT OTHER LOCATIONS

# YOUR DRUM SOUND

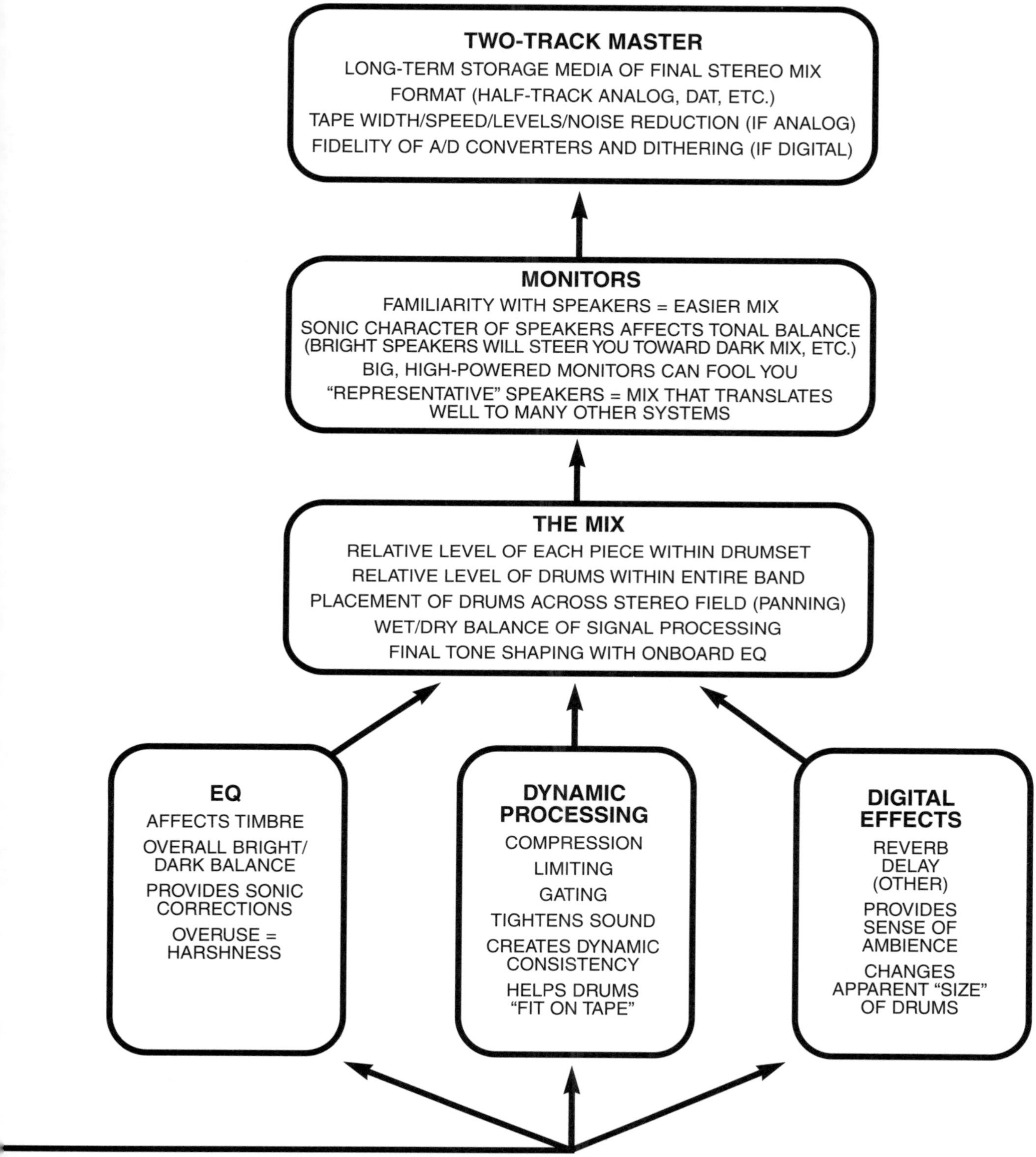

**TWO-TRACK MASTER**
LONG-TERM STORAGE MEDIA OF FINAL STEREO MIX
FORMAT (HALF-TRACK ANALOG, DAT, ETC.)
TAPE WIDTH/SPEED/LEVELS/NOISE REDUCTION (IF ANALOG)
FIDELITY OF A/D CONVERTERS AND DITHERING (IF DIGITAL)

↑

**MONITORS**
FAMILIARITY WITH SPEAKERS = EASIER MIX
SONIC CHARACTER OF SPEAKERS AFFECTS TONAL BALANCE
(BRIGHT SPEAKERS WILL STEER YOU TOWARD DARK MIX, ETC.)
BIG, HIGH-POWERED MONITORS CAN FOOL YOU
"REPRESENTATIVE" SPEAKERS = MIX THAT TRANSLATES
WELL TO MANY OTHER SYSTEMS

↑

**THE MIX**
RELATIVE LEVEL OF EACH PIECE WITHIN DRUMSET
RELATIVE LEVEL OF DRUMS WITHIN ENTIRE BAND
PLACEMENT OF DRUMS ACROSS STEREO FIELD (PANNING)
WET/DRY BALANCE OF SIGNAL PROCESSING
FINAL TONE SHAPING WITH ONBOARD EQ

**EQ**
AFFECTS TIMBRE
OVERALL BRIGHT/
DARK BALANCE
PROVIDES SONIC
CORRECTIONS
OVERUSE =
HARSHNESS

**DYNAMIC
PROCESSING**
COMPRESSION
LIMITING
GATING
TIGHTENS SOUND
CREATES DYNAMIC
CONSISTENCY
HELPS DRUMS
"FIT ON TAPE"

**DIGITAL
EFFECTS**
REVERB
DELAY
(OTHER)
PROVIDES
SENSE OF
AMBIENCE
CHANGES
APPARENT "SIZE"
OF DRUMS

Even though there are a lot of different points on the chart, it only lists fairly major factors. (We could get into details like the relative merits of different types of cables, but we'll leave that to the pocket-protector crowd. We just want to exercise reasonable care.) In our little recording session scenario we managed to violate almost everything on the chart (and I've seen situations almost this bad in real life), so it's no wonder we probably wouldn't be pleased with the results. What we're going to do in the following chapters is look at each of these factors in detail and get some practical advice about their application. For now, however, I want to reduce all these variables into a few categories:

1. You
2. Your instrument
3. The room
4. The recording equipment
5. Engineering and production decisions

The hardware (items 2, 3, and 4) is important, but the really critical stuff is in the first and last items: the "human factor." (Notice that most of the problems in our imaginary session were really due to the attitude and decisions of the people involved.)

A great drummer and a talented engineer can get together in a small room with a simple drumkit and modest, project-studio-type equipment and create professional-sounding drum tracks. (In fact, this is exactly what's happening these days with many independent label recordings.) Conversely, if you're a drummer with a sloppy attitude towards your playing and your instrument, and you're working with a similarly lazy engineer, the finest equipment in the world isn't going to help you.

Another concept to keep in mind is the idea that a chain is only as strong as its weakest link. As applied to recording drums, this means that if you let something bad happen to your sound at one stage, doing things perfectly at every other stage will not make up for it. As tempting as the idea is, don't ever count on "fixing it in the mix"—that's largely a myth. If you become unhappy with your sound at any point, from the initial sound of your drums in the room to the final EQ tweaks during the mix, don't proceed to the next step until you diagnose the current problem and fix it.

Now let's look at some overall guidelines to follow on the path towards a righteous drum sound.

# CHAPTER 2

# The Ten Commandments Of Recording Drums

It's a cliché, but it's true: Knowledge *is* power. The more you know about the way things work inside the studio, the less your drum sound will be at the mercy of other people (who are most likely *not* drummers). Here, then, are the ten commandments of recording drums (which, unlike the originals, aren't written in stone, but they'll provide a starting point).

1. **Thou Shalt Define Thy Drum Sound**. Before you can *get* what you want, you have to *know* what you want, so this is where it all starts. Before you tune your drums, select which cymbals to use, or do anything else, you should have an answer to the question: "How do I envision my drum sound on the finished recording?"

Drum sound is a personal thing, and it contributes greatly to your identity as a drummer. So it's worth some serious consideration. Your personal taste goes a long way in deciding this, of course, as does the style of music you're playing. We generally expect a different drum sound on a rock recording than on a big band one, for example, but this convention is changing. I've heard alternative bands using drums that sound like a wide-open jazz kit (and it works!). Anything goes in your quest for your signature sound, as long as you and your band feel it's musically appropriate for the situation. (There is an exception to this, which we'll cover in commandment #3.)

2. **Thou Shalt Communicate Thy Vision**. Once you get in the studio it's up to you to see that the engineer has a clear idea of how you want your drums to sound. To effectively convey your ideas, it's helpful to know certain terms (which we'll cover later on). It's usually not enough to say, "I want a big, full drum sound." (After all, who doesn't?)

One way around this is to bring in recorded examples of drum tracks similar to your ideal sound. Here, too, any additional details you can add will only help your cause (such as saying, "I like the drums on this CD, but I'd like my snare to be brighter and have less reverb on it."). Also, don't worry that you'll sound exactly like the drummer in your examples. There are so many variables involved that you'll still sound unique—but at least the engineer will have a clue as to what to aim for.

Why not simply request that your drums sound on tape the way they do live? Some engineers suggest that you try this approach, but what they mean is "get your drums sounding as good as you can in the room and I'll get a sound in the control room that captures the *character* of your live drums." In actuality, your drums *can't* sound on tape exactly the way they do live. Part of the reason is that no drum can be said to have *one* specific sound. It depends on your perspective. When *you* hear your kit, you're sitting on top of it with your ears approximately 24" from the snare. Others usually hear it from out front, several feet away. In the studio it will be "heard" by several mic's, some of them across the room and some of them within inches of individual drums. Each location yields a very different perception of the sound from the same instrument. There are numerous other artifices introduced in the recording process (to say nothing of the fact that we listen to recordings through speakers), all of which add up to the fact that there are going to be differences between your acoustic drum sound and your recorded drum sound. It's up to you to make sure that these differences benefit rather than hurt your sound.

3. **Thou Shalt Remain Flexible**. Time for a reality check. If someone else (bandmember, engineer, producer, etc.) suggests a change in your sound, by all means *give it a try*. They may well be right, and even if they aren't you may learn something in the process. When the writer of the song being recorded has an opinion about the drums, I give it more weight, because it's that writer's baby. Just as you have to be an advocate for *your* sound, the writer has an obligation to try to see that *his* or *her* original vision of the song is realized, and you should respect that.

When you're paying for studio time to make a tape, you are the client and you call the shots regarding creative decisions. It's when the money flows in the opposite direction that we encounter the exception mentioned earlier. If someone's hiring you to play on a given project, you certainly can (and should) offer suggestions that you think will benefit the music. But in the end the person who hired you has the final say. As a professional, you should do your best to provide what he or she wants. We'll talk a little more about this in Chapter 10.

4. **Thou Shalt Know Thy Recording Gear**. Equalizers, reverbs, compressors, noise gates, and other processing gear can be your friends—*if* you understand how they work. They can really save the day when a problem arises, but if they're misused (or overused) they can ruin your drum tracks.

Want your 5" snare to sound like a deep snare (or a piccolo)? Want to smooth out some unevenness in your bass drum dynamics, or keep that big reverb on your snare from turning your hi-hats into a muddy wash of noise? This and much more can be accomplished with processors and effects, but you have to have a clue as to how they work. You don't have to be an expert on using this gear; that's the

engineer's job. You just have to know enough to suggest, "Why don't we use some frequency-dependent gating to keep that snare bleed out of my kick track?" The engineer will do the rest.

5. **Thou Shalt Choose Thy Microphones Wisely**. The perfectly transparent microphone doesn't exist...and if it did, you probably wouldn't like its sound! Truthfully, every microphone is a complex equalizer that colors your sound—sometimes slightly and sometimes in obvious ways. The trick is to use mic's that color the sound in ways beneficial to the job at hand.

Imagine a mic' with a beefy low-end response, a flat or slightly suppressed lower midrange, a peak in the upper mids, and the very high end rolled off. Such a mic' would sound terrible on your cymbals, rendering them thick and clanky—but it might be absolutely *killer* on your kick or large toms. The same story applies to mic' *placement*: identical mic's can sound totally different in different locations. We'll cover all this in detail later, but the point is that mic's make a huge difference, and before you start adding EQ to "fix" a sound, it's preferable to try different miking schemes.

6. **Thou Shalt Select Thy Room With Care**. Drums, mic's, and recording gear are all parts of a "system," with each component affecting your final sound. Well, the room you're recording in is yet another part of the system, and it can make a substantial difference in the end result.

Each room has its own sonic personality, dictated by its size, geometry, construction, surface coverings, and the presence or absence of objects within the room. We'll discuss each of these variables in Chapter 4 (along with some solutions to "problem rooms"), but here are a few guidelines for those who can't wait to start recording.

The easiest way to tell if a room will work for recording drums is simply to set up the basics (kick/snare/hats) and *play*. Does it sound good from behind the drums...from out front...from across the room...and most importantly, from in the control room? Only you can decide what's right for your music, but a good room can usually be fairly ambient as long as it has an even distribution of highs, mids, and lows. Hard surfaces (like glass, tile, or plaster) reflect high frequencies, while softer materials (such as carpet, curtains, or foam) absorb them. Both of these types of materials can be added or removed to balance the room. Large rooms have a longer decay, adding "air" to the sound, while small rooms (especially live ones) have a shorter, "in your face" type of reverberance. Everything else being equal, a room with a higher ceiling usually has a bigger and warmer sound. Rooms having two or more dimensions of equal length (i.e. squares or cubes) will have an artificial boost at the resonant frequency. There are lots of formulae used to determine what will or won't work, but above all else: Use your ears!

### 7. Thou Shalt Keep Thy Drums Sounding Good.

The drums themselves are another key part of the recording chain, and it's axiomatic in the recording industry that a good-sounding tape starts with a good-sounding instrument.

We'll be hearing from some experts on this, discussing subjects like head selection, tuning, muffling, and drum preparation. In general, you want to keep in mind the idea that there are different priorities in the studio versus the stage. Live (especially in unmiked situations), volume and projection are important, and we don't worry too much about small noises in the kit, overly ringy drums, or snare buzz. (Plus, a large kit can add visual impact to your live act.)

In the studio, however, *tone production* is paramount, along with all the ancillary things that go into it. Non-musical noises should be eliminated, and since we can't *see* the drumset on a tape there's no reason to use more gear than is needed for the song at hand. (In fact, there are some very real benefits to only using what you need, as we'll see.)

### 8. Thou Shalt Play Not For Thyself But For Thy Tape.

Analogous to the point made above, there are different priorities when you're playing in the studio. Small clams that you can ignore in the heat of a live performance will return to haunt you (over and over!) on tape. Things like a missed rimshot or a stick click are much more exposed, so precision is necessary. But more important than any of this is the concept of *playing for the tape*. This means constructing parts that support the song, rather than trying to show off all your chops at once.

I've been convinced through watching and listening to great drummers that one of the keys to a successful recording is solid, supportive playing that makes the music feel good. *Time* and *groove*, right?

This doesn't mean you shouldn't pull off some serious chops when the tune calls for it, but rather that their use should be dictated by the music and not your ego.

### 9. Thou Shalt Ask Many Questions.

If you pay for studio time and all you come away with is a tape, you didn't really get your money's worth. One of the best places to learn about recording drums is in the studio, from the guy who does it for a living.

Without being a pest, ask the engineer what he's doing and why. You'll find that most engineers are only too happy to talk about their craft with an interested person. Watch everything that goes on, and *take notes*. (I did this when I started, and it helped me enormously.) One of the best things about this type of knowledge is that it's portable. Somewhere down the road you might have a problem in a different studio, and you can suggest something you picked up during a previous session.

### 10. Thou Shalt Keep A Positive Attitude.

This is *key*. Negativity is contagious and only serves to bring down everyone you're working with. This, in turn, makes it almost impossible to achieve anything worthwhile. A positive attitude, on the other hand, can really open doors to creativity.

A recent survey of successful entrepreneurs revealed that the quality they looked for most when hiring—over intelligence, business acumen, or a higher education—was *enthusiasm*. I agree. When looking for musicians, I'll take a "good" player with an enthusiastic, positive attitude over a "great" player with a poor attitude every time—and so will a lot of other folks. When problems arise (as they occasionally do), be a "problem solver" instead of a complainer, and things will get back in the groove that much quicker.

# CHAPTER 3

# Equipment Selection And Preparation

You've heard it before: A good-sounding recording starts with a good-sounding instrument. So before we go any further we're going to discuss getting your drumset ready for the studio.

**Prior to entering the studio, dismantle your drums. Check the bearing edges, tighten all fasteners, pack lugs (if necessary), and generally be sure that the drum is in the best possible condition.**

First, let's dispel the myth that you have to have an expensive, custom-made set of thin-shelled, all-maple or birch drums (approximate value = 1 new car) in order to get a "pro" drum sound on record. *Not true.* While there are many benefits to owning a fine instrument, I firmly believe that any kit currently made by any of the "name" manufacturers (including their budget-minded "import" models) has the potential to make a professional recording—assuming you do your part to optimize that kit's sound. With that in mind, let's look at what we can do to improve the situation, starting with some trouble spots.

## Troubleshooting

Before we attempt to tweak a drum's sound, we need to ensure that the drum itself is in good mechanical condition. Otherwise we could waste a lot of time trying different heads and/or tunings on a drum that's not going to sound good until it gets some repair.

**Shells**. If a drum tunes up easily, stays in tune, and delivers a smooth, sustaining pitch, then the shell probably doesn't have any fundamental problems. If the drum *won't* do these things, however, a good place to start would be to check the bearing edges. Pop the heads off and inspect the edges, looking for any obvious defects (such as voids in the plies). Run your finger around the edges, feeling for any little bumps or depressions. Check for flatness by placing the shell on a flat surface (like glass or marble) and looking for any gaps. Any flaws revealed by these checks need to be addressed by a competent repair shop; re-cutting bearing edges is not a job for amateurs. Also check problem drums for roundness. A lopsided shell isn't going to produce a clear pitch until it gets some serious help.

**Hardware**. Hoops, like bearing edges, should be flat. If you have one that's slightly warped you can usually bend it back into shape, but one that's badly bent or dented should be replaced. Tension casings should be snugly fastened to the shell with no play, and their threads should be clean and free of any debris that could prevent smooth tightening of the tension rods. To clean up the threads pick up a #12 x 24 tap at the hardware store and run it through each lug. Tension rods should likewise be straight and clean and able to tighten smoothly without binding. Any that don't meet this criteria should be replaced.

**Noises**. There may be certain noises (non-musical sounds) produced by your drumset that, while not particularly bothersome in a live situation, could present a problem under the scrutiny of the recording studio. Ross Garfield ("The Drum Doctor") is well-known for his expertise in prepping drums for the studio. Here are some of his tips for eliminating noises in the drumkit.

"Bring a can of *WD-40* to eliminate squeaks," says Ross. "In fact, if you can apply it to the drumset *before* going in the studio, that's even better. Another thing you should do well in advance is make sure your lugs are packed. You'd be surprised at what a weird sound they can make otherwise. A lot of times a producer will call me and say, 'Have you ever heard this sound before? Whenever we hit the bass drum it sounds like there's a tambourine going off!' And we'll say, 'Oh, sure, those are the lugs. The springs inside are vibrating. You have to take each one off and pack it with cotton.' They won't have time to do that, so they end up having to rent one of *our* bass drums, which

already have the lugs packed."

Okay—your drums are mechanically sound, and all the rattles and squeaks have been taken care of. Now let's talk about getting the best sound possible out of your kit.

## Heads

This is a biggie. The type (or types) of heads you select, their condition, and the way you tune them will have more of an effect on the acoustic sound of your drums than any other factor. Regardless of the type of sound you're going for, fresh heads are a *must*. Worn heads that are stretched or dented won't let your drums respond properly and will only hinder you in the studio.

Bob Gatzen is a designer and consultant for Evans drumheads and for Noble & Cooley drums (as well as being a drummer, composer, producer, and studio owner). He offers some wisdom about an often-overlooked aspect of changing heads.

"If you're going in the studio," says Bob, "replace all the heads—especially the *bottom* heads. You can

Fresh drumheads are a must for any recording project.

make a drumset sound like brand-new if you replace the bottom heads. *Not* replacing them is the biggest mistake drummers make. They feel that since bottom heads don't get dented, they can last forever. But bottom heads ought to be changed a couple times a year, because polyester film dries out and loses its resiliency. As a result, you can't get the drum tuned down low. To get the head to work correctly you usually end up tuning the bottom head too high, because it's unforgiving and has lost its 'bounce.' If drummers replace the bottom heads just a day or two before going into the studio, they'll often be amazed. The kit will feel new again, and it will sound fresh."

The *type* of head to use is largely a personal decision, but there are a few things to keep in mind. The first is that you shouldn't make a radical change right before you go into the studio in the hope that it'll improve your sound. It's hard enough to "be yourself" in a recording situation without having to worry about your drums sounding and feeling completely different than what you're used to. Go with what's been working for you. If you're not happy with your current choice of heads, experiment with different models well in advance of entering the studio. This will not only give you time to get used to them, but will allow you to ensure that their sound works well in the context of the music you'll be playing.

Another consideration is that in the studio, things like *durability* and *volume* are less of a priority than they are on stage. *Tone production* becomes the paramount issue. So you can get away with using thinner heads than you might take on the road (assuming you like the sound and response of them). Kenny Aronoff, for example, swaps his coated *Emperors* for coated *Ambassadors* when he's going in the studio.

## Tuning

The same general rules apply with tuning as with head selection. You're asking for trouble if you completely revamp your overall tuning scheme the night before you hit the studio. Instead, try to make each drum sound as good as it can within the general range you're used to playing it in. The important thing is to make sure there are no "sour" overtones emanating from any of your drums, and that they *feel* good to you.

Most of you have probably established a fixed tuning procedure that works for you. If so, you should stick with it. But if you're inexperienced and don't know where to start, here are some very basic guidelines.

Let's assume we're starting with a tom. Put fresh heads on the drum, top and bottom. Medium-weight, single-ply heads work well if you like an open sound and you aren't going to play extremely hard. (For less ring or for heavy hitters, use a double-ply or edge-damped head on top, but leave the single-ply head on the bottom.)

Tighten both heads well beyond normal playing tension, and let them sit that way for a while (to seat the head against the bearing edge). Then loosen them to where the tension rods spin freely. Place the drum on a carpeted floor or some other surface that will stop the bottom head from vibrating. Tighten the top tension rods until they touch the hoop. Then, following a star pattern (like tightening lug nuts on a wheel), tighten the rods until the head has just enough tension to produce a sustained pitch. Go around the drum, lightly tapping the head an inch in from each lug. Fine tune each rod until they all produce the same pitch on the head. Now go around the drum again and raise the tension at each rod slightly (and always the same amount at each rod) so that the overall pitch comes up about a half step. (We're shooting for a middle-of-the-road sound that will work in a variety of situations.)

Turn the drum upside-down and follow the same procedure with the bottom head, ending up with the same pitch on both heads. This will give you maximum volume and sustain from the drum while producing a pure, open tone. If you want some pitch bend (at the sacrifice of a small amount of sustain), raise the bottom head a half step above the top head. This is only a rough guide; you'll obviously have to experiment with various tunings to dial in your preferred sound. But probably more important than the exact pitch you choose is the need for the drum to be in tune with itself (even tension at each lug). An out-of-tune drum can generate some pretty awful "wang"-type overtones that are hard to get rid of once they're on tape. (Similar sour tones can be caused by worn-out, dented heads—no matter *how* carefully they're tuned. So do yourself a favor and have fresh, well-tuned heads on your toms prior to the session.)

Kick drums are approached differently than toms, with their tuning and muffling more style-dependent. For most types of contemporary music you're usually better off using a damped head with minimal muffling than an undamped head and tons of muffling, so I like heads like the Remo *Powerstroke 3* or the Evans *EQ3* on a kick. Tune the batter head fairly loose. (Not so slack that it wrinkles, but about as low as it'll go and still hold a tone.) This will help the beater attack. Bring the front head up a bit higher so you can get some resonance from it. A hole in the front head is necessary to get a mic' inside (unless you're using something like the May internal mic's), but it should be off-center and as small as possible so it doesn't kill the sustain. (Various manufacturers make front heads with small offset holes already in place.) If you want a bass drum with a little ambience, this combination of head type and tuning sounds great by itself (with no muffling). If you want more control, you can add one of the pads from Evans or DW (or whatever dampening you choose).

Snare tuning is a highly personal matter, since the snare is usually the signature voice in a drumset. So consider the following as merely a jumping-off point from which you should experiment. Start with fresh heads—a 3 mil snare-side head and a 10 mil, single-ply batter head (I like a white coated *Ambassador*) work well for most applications. I prefer no built-in dampening on snare heads *for studio use* because I want the option of varying the amount of overtones at a moment's notice.

For metal drums, start with the bottom head "tight" and the top head "medium-tight," then tighten up the snare wires until their response is crisp (but not so tight that they choke the drum). With wood drums I like both heads to be somewhat tighter than on a metal drum due to the character imparted by a wooden shell. (A too-tight metal snare can come off as harsh and thin, while a wood drum tuned to the same tension is likely to exhibit a lively "pop" that records well.) Obviously, if you're looking for a nice "fatback" snare sound you'll want to use a deeper-shelled drum with a substantially lower pitch and probably more dampening—while with a piccolo you'd use the opposite approach.

In keeping with the philosophy of "get the right sound at the source rather than trying to beat it into shape later," here are a couple more snare ideas. To increase the crispness of the snare sound, swap the standard 20-strand snare wires for 40-strand models. To increase rimshot volume and overall projection, put a die-cast hoop on the drum. And for more "cut" through a dense mix, think

small rather than big. What I mean is, if your 7"-deep snare is getting lost, try a 5" or less. In fact, piccolo snares translate very well to tape, as do 13"-diameter drums.

Again, this whole area is very subjective, and if you're considering new tuning schemes you should experiment with them *prior* to any recording projects. For further help in this area check out Richard Watson's excellent "Guide To Drumset Tuning" feature in the March '94 issue of *Modern Drummer*. Bob Gatzen also has a comprehensive video on this subject called *Drum Tuning: Sound And Design* (DCI Video), which I highly recommend.

## Muffling

The rule for muffling is the same as for heads and tuning: Unless you're a hired gun being paid to create a specific sound that the producer desires, don't automatically change the way you normally do business just because you're in the studio. If you run your kit onstage without much muffling, then that's the configuration to use *as a starting point* in the studio (assuming *you* like the sound you've been getting). The reason I use the phrase "starting point" is because, as we've mentioned before, things sound different to a microphone an inch from a drum than from several feet away. When you hear the first takes played back in the control room you may want to make some adjustments, so arrive prepared.

My general feeling with toms is that the best way to control the tone is with head selection rather than with outright muffling. If a single-ply head gives you too much ring, you can use a single-ply with a built-in dampening ring near the edge, or a double-ply, or a double-ply with a ring, or with dots, etc. This gives you several options toward getting the amount of dampening you want without destroying the feel of the drum. You also get a better tone using a damped head than a single-ply head with lots of stuff taped to it. A damped head has a more subtle effect on the sound, and the sustain seems smoother. Of course there are exceptions, but a lot of times it seems like the less dampening the better, and (as long as the music calls for it) it's hard to beat the wide-open sound of single-ply heads on the top and bottom.

The primary focus regarding actual muffling will be the bass drum—and, to a lesser extent, the snare. Bring the drum the way you normally use it, but also bring various types of muffling so you have several *different* options immediately available in the studio. For the kick drum you might consider bringing a rolled-up towel, a down pillow, a packing blanket, and maybe a pad like an Evans *EQ Pad* or a Drum Workshop *Bass Drum Pillow*. It's also a good idea to have a couple of different beaters—one hard and one soft—so you can vary the amount of attack if you so desire. For the snare there are countless options, both commercial and homemade. Some of my favorites are the *Mylar* "donuts" made by different manufacturers. They're available in various widths, so you can go from just a little dampening to almost complete elimination of the overtones without affecting the feel of the playing surface. And speaking of snares, this is a good time to talk about...

> **Any kit has the potential to make a professional recording—assuming you do your part to optimize that kit's sound.**

## Snare Buzz

The reason I didn't put this under the *noises* section is that I don't really think of snare buzz as a noise as much as part of the "ambience" of the drumset. (In fact, if I play a kick drum with the nearby snare turned off it doesn't sound quite right to me.) But some folks are concerned about it, so it needs to be addressed.

First off, don't go crazy taping up the bottom of your snare drum trying to get rid of all traces of sympathetic buzz. If you ever actually accomplished this (which is doubtful) you'd probably hate the sound of your drum, and it really isn't necessary. I've almost never heard snare buzz so bad that it became objectionable in the final mix. Sure, you can hear it if you solo the snare track, but once the other instruments and vocals are added it usually becomes insignificant. An exception might be during an exposed part of a quiet ballad, but even here there are things you can do short of choking the drum. By far the worst type of snare buzz is the long, sustained buzzing caused by other instruments, and in the studio there are several cures for this that aren't available on stage.

Let's say certain notes on the bass guitar are causing the snares to resonate (which is a common problem). You could place the bass amp in an isolation booth, a closet, in the control room, or down

the hall. You could record the bass direct (without speakers) by going through a direct box or a preamp, then into the board. You could track the bass at a different time than the drums. In a worst-case scenario you could gate the snare during the exposed section—but I'd recommend doing that *only* if the snare part was very simple and only if there were *no* other options.

If other drums in your set are causing snare buzz, you can locate and detune the offending drum(s). You can also decrease snare sensitivity by loosening the tension rods on the bottom head adjacent to the snare wires. But before I did either of these things I'd want to be certain the buzz was going to be audible—and objectionable—within the context of the entire band.

## Cymbals

Except for cleaning them, about all you can do for cymbals in the studio is to decide which ones to use and where to place them—both of which can have a bigger effect than you might think. The potential problem here is "splatter," which is what happens when the high-frequency energy from the cymbals overpowers everything else, turning your drum sound into an indistinct, splashy mess. Part of the solution, of course, is not to bash the daylights out of your cymbals when you're recording. But you can also get some help from the proper *selection* of cymbals to use on a given project.

You may use half a dozen crash cymbals onstage, but looks don't count in the studio and volume is not a high priority. So consider limiting yourself to your smaller, thinner cymbals. They'll sound better on tape, they'll blend better with the rest of your drumset, and they won't splatter over the rest of the mix.

As for *placement* of the cymbals, check out Rod Morgenstein's comments (at the end of this chapter) regarding keeping cymbals from bleeding into the rest of the kit. It's up to you to decide if you want to raise your cymbals to keep the bleed down, but it's certainly a great idea to keep in your bag of tricks in case you ever encounter this particular problem during a session.

Actually, there *is* something (besides cleaning) that you can do to change the sound of your cymbals: You can change your sticks. A bigger stick will obviously generate more volume than a smaller one. But there are more subtle changes you can make, as well. For instance, two sticks of the same size—but with different tip shapes—will produce different sounds from the same cymbal. (And if I *really* want a brighter ping out of a ride cymbal, I'll switch to nylon tips.) This underscores the advantage of keeping a variety of sticks in your bag.

## The Drumset Itself

Let's spend a minute talking about the size of your kit—not the dimensions of the individual drums, but the total number of pieces. Everything else being equal, a smaller kit will record better than a big one. Why? On a four-piece kit you'll have one mic' on the kick, one on the snare, one on the hi-hats, one on each of two toms, and a pair of overheads. On a nine-piece kit you'll have the same mic's, plus a mic' on the second kick and *four more* tom mic's. All those extra open mic's are going to spend 99% of their time doing nothing but picking up bleed from the "core" of the kit (kick/snare/hats), making it that much harder to get a great drum sound.

If you're going to actually *use* everything on your kit, great. But if not, you can do without all the open mic's. I'm *not* saying not to bring your whole kit. If it makes you happy, then bring it, set it up, mic' everything, and get levels. But when you realize that on a certain song you're only going to use one of your toms, do yourself a favor and tell the engineer. He'll have the option of shutting down the other tom mic's, making things sound that much cleaner (and saving a few tape tracks in the process). And, if the *whole project* only requires a basic kit, you'll be time and money ahead to just set up what you need (fewer mic's for the engineer to set up, fewer levels to set, less time spent tweaking equalizers and other processors for each drum, etc.). The mix will go that much faster, too.

We've covered quite a few things you can do to tweak your set into perfection—all of which will definitely help your recordings sound better. But perhaps the most important aspect of having a good-sounding drumset is that it *feels good* when you play, inspiring you on to new heights of creativity.

## Ask The Pros

### Drum Prep

**Q. Let's talk about your drums for a minute. Do you do anything to your kit to get it ready for the studio as opposed to the stage?**

**Kenny Aronoff:** The first thing is the heads. I'll put white coated *Ambassadors* on top of the toms and the snare, and sometimes on the bass drum. Lately I've been using the Remo *Powerstroke 3* clear head both live and in the studio on the bass drum. Sometimes, if I'm playing rock 'n' roll, I'll use an *Ambassador* head with a black dot underneath the head—just for a little more reinforcement. It muffles a little bit, but not enough to create a problem. Live, I'll use clear *Emperors* on the toms and a coated *Emperor* on the snare—only for the added endurance.

**Gregg Bissonette:** I tune my drums about the same, whether live or in the studio: fat tones with lots of attack. Sometimes I might use a 16" floor tom instead of an 18", depending on the music. I use white coated *Ambassadors* on the tops and clear *Ambassadors* on the bottoms, and I tune them to the same pitch. That way the drums really resonate. I don't like a felt beater on my bass drum, so I use the hard-plastic side of a DW beater. If I'm hitting my bass drum with a piece of cotton or felt it's going to go *whoomp-whoomp*. I'd rather have the attack of the bass drum sound similar to the attack of the toms, which I'm hitting with a stick.

**Jim Keltner:** I don't play live that often. When I do I generally play the same drums I use in the studio. If it's a different set of drums, they're tuned the same way. I run my drums pretty wide open now—although it didn't always used to be that way. A drum is meant to go *boom* or *bang*; it's not meant to go *bap*. If you're going to do that you might as well use a cardboard box.

**Rod Morgenstein:** One thing I definitely do differently in the studio is raise all of my cymbals higher. I can remember actually *lunging* for the crash cymbals on one session, because the engineer said, "The further you can get them away from the toms, the easier it's going to be for me to deal with making your kit sound real good." It's terrible if you listen back to a track and the cymbals are just too loud—but there's nothing you can do about it after the fact. A lot of people don't like to have to reach for things, so they keep them pretty low. But I'll play them a little bit higher than normal to help the recording process.

I've tried to lower the tuning of my toms to get deeper tones—but I've found that I kind of like it better pitching them higher. You can have a bunch of toms, but if there's not a big pitch difference in them you'll be listening back to this lick that you thought sounded really cool and it won't *sound* like all those different toms. I try to make a habit of tuning the lowest floor tom as *low* as it'll go without losing its tone, and tuning the highest rack tom up—not sounding like a bongo, but pretty damn high—to get as wide a pitch differentiation as possible. On the road, it might not be quite as drastic.

Sometimes you get these horrible rings and you have to do a little dampening. That happens much more in the studio than live. I hardly ever put anything on a tom-tom when I play live. The snare has a muffling ring of some sort on it. But in the studio there are definitely times when napkins and duct tape or whatever are brought out, and you start playing around with individual tom-toms just to get a little bit of that ring out of them.

**Simon Phillips:** I have a range of snare drums, and in the studio I might pick up another snare drum and change it over if I don't think the first one sounded very good for that song. For the bass drum, maybe I'll dampen the front head a little bit if there's too much sustain on the drum.

I also vary my playing for each song, which can change the way the drums sound. And as I change my playing, the engineer should chase me. He should go, "Okay, he's hitting the snare drum quieter now. Let's turn the kick up, let's change the balance of everything"—which will make the kit appear to sound different. So, yeah, there are those changes.

There are also the changes where the producer may ask for a certain kind of sound. He'll say, "Listen, I've been checking the sound and it's really not what I'm thinking of. Can we try something like *this*?" And I'll say, "Okay, let's see how it goes."

**J.R. Robinson:** I don't do anything differently between playing live and recording. I remember when I first got to Los Angeles in 1978, the studio guys told me, "You have to tune the drums totally differently...use different heads..." and all this stuff. I'd been playing live for so many years that I said, "Wait a second here. I'm not buying that." It took me playing on the road *and* in the studio to see that when you put a mic' on a drum you should first tune that drum correctly. You can't get a great drum sound unless the drums are tuned correctly. Then when you bring the drum up in the mix it should sound like who you are.

I use Remo coated *Emperors* on the tops of my toms and clear *Ambassadors* on the bottoms. Lately on the kick I've been using the Remo *Powerstroke 3*, but normally I use an *Ambassador* coated or clear on the beater side. And I always use a front head on the bass drum, with a small hole to get the mic' in. If I'm using an *Ambassador*, I'll cut a packing blanket into fourths and just lay it flat into the bed of the bass drum so that it touches maybe two inches up on either head. I also have an old Rufus sandbag about which I'm kind of sentimental. I don't know if it really makes a difference or not, but we set it in the middle of the bass drum. [laughs]

**Q. To make your job easier as an engineer, what should drummers know when they go into the studio besides how to play the drums?**

**Mike Fraser:** The first thing is the selection of drumheads, depending on what kind of sound is desired. Then how the drums are tuned is really critical, because if the drum doesn't sound good, there's nothing an engineer can do.

**Ed Thacker:** It's good when drummers have a sense of tuning. In other words they know how to tune drums and it's *important* to them—not just "tighten it up and hit it." The other most important thing is understanding an inner sense of dynamics when they're playing. With some drummers, that right arm is a lot stronger than that left arm [laughs]— and that's the "bash" concept. It makes my job a lot easier when the drummer understands the relationship of the dynamics when he or she is hitting the cymbals as compared to the snare or the toms—hitting the drums so they *speak*.

# CHAPTER

# The Room

Even though the study of acoustics is a science, the definition of a good room is still largely subjective. A "good room" is simply one that works for the type of recording you wish to make. The trick is in identifying such a room prior to investing your time and money. And to complicate matters even further, a good recording *can* be made in almost any room, if need be.

That said, this chapter should be over, right? Not so fast. Wasn't it stated in an earlier chapter that if need be, good music can be made on any drumset? Yes—but that doesn't mean that we don't care about the quality of our drums, what kind of heads we use, how they're tuned, etc. The proper instrument makes it easier for us to fully realize our musical vision, sounds more musical to both us and the listener, is a joy to play on, and may even inspire us to greater creativity. Well, all of the above also applies to the proper room for one simple reason: Drums are an acoustic instrument, and *the room is part of the instrument.*

Unless you're playing in an anechoic chamber or outside on a completely sound-absorbing stage

with no structures nearby, a good part of your drum sound—for better or worse—is a product of the environment you're in. To get an approximation of just how true this is, take your snare out to the middle of a large grassy area away from any buildings (the top of a small hill is best) and play it. Even better (though a bit more cumbersome) is to bring your kick drum: You'll be amazed at how incredibly thin and dry it sounds. Well, the difference between

**A project studio (such as Sonny Ryan's Cave Studio, shown here) is the most compact recording space, and may not even allow for recording live drums.**

Hollywood's Ocean Way studios offer state-of-the art acoustic design...

surface in question. Hard, flat surfaces will reflect sound in the same way a mirror or piece of polished marble will reflect light. Surfaces with many different planes and angles will diffuse the sound, much like a wrinkled piece of aluminum foil will diffuse light shone upon it. (The light will still be reflected, but the reflections will be jumbled up in different directions rather than the coherent reflections you get from a mirror.) Soft, porous surfaces (especially those with depth, like corrugated foam) will absorb and dissipate sound the way black velvet will absorb light.

It should be noted that these descriptions are more applicable to mid and high frequencies than to low frequencies, which behave differently due to their extremely long wavelengths. Because of this, a room can be "tuned" by the addition of various materials to bring the high end in line with the low end (which is more a factor of the geometry and construction of the room itself than surface coverings). One of the adverse factors affecting the low end is the presence of *resonant frequencies*. These occur when two or more dimensions of a room are the same or multiples of each other. When this happens, a frequency that has a wavelength equal to the common room dimension gets boosted by the room, resulting in a (usually) unwanted peak in the frequency response. For example, a room that's 20' x 20' with a 10'

this papery little sound and the full sound you're used to hearing from your drum is strictly due to the absence of any *reflected sound*, which is usually a prominent component of a drum's overall sound. What's left is the *direct sound*, and its anemic condition (without benefit of any reflections) tells us just how important the room's contribution really is.

As we'll see, the room acts as both an equalizer *and* a reverb. In later chapters we'll learn that EQ can change the perceived depth of a drum (by accentuating or reducing either fundamentals or harmonics), while reverb adds ambience (varying the apparent size and liveliness of the sound). The wrong room can fight your enhancements every step of the way, making it difficult to achieve your desired sound. But the right room will work with you—sometimes to the point where you can just about put up the mic's and play. How do rooms acquire their different sonic personalities? Let's peek inside the soundwaves for a minute and see.

## Physics

Surfaces affect soundwaves by either *reflecting*, *diffusing*, or *absorbing* them (or some combination of these) depending on the nature of the

...along with size and technical sophistication.

ceiling will have a resonant frequency of around 55 Hz, which will cause the room to "boom" every time your bass player hits his low A. Far better would be a room that was, say, 17' x 25' with the same 10' ceiling. That room's fundamental frequencies would be staggered (44 Hz, 65 Hz, and 110 Hz) for a smoother low end.

Another possible adverse condition is the presence of *flutter echoes*. These can happen when parallel reflective surfaces (such as hard walls) face each other across the room. What happens is that sounds bounce back and forth between the walls, creating a rapid series of short echoes that decay away, sounding "fluttery." Flutter echoes are more noticeable with short percussive sounds, so they're particularly aggravating to drummers. A similar problem is the *slapback* echo, caused by sound coming back from a single hard surface (usually the far wall) resulting in a single echo— reminiscent of the sound on old rockabilly recordings. A quick check for these problems is to stand between the walls and clap your hands, listening for their characteristic sounds.

A small-scale commercial studio (such as the author's Polar Productions facility) will be limited in equipment and space, but can still accommodate a kit.

Besides having a certain timbre (brighter or darker, depending on which frequencies the room accentuates or absorbs), rooms also have a quantity of overall reverberation known as the RT-60. We'll talk about this more when we get into digital effects, but the RT-60 is basically how long it takes a reverb to decay to the point of inaudibility. (Although usually measured irrespective of frequency content, a brighter room will *seem* more ambient than a darker room even though they may have identical RT-60s.) The easiest way to determine a room's decay time is to make short sounds (clap your hands or hit a damped snare) and listen for how long the sound seems to hang in the air.

That's enough theory for now. Let's get down to some practical realities.

## Ambience Considerations

The first step when looking for a room is to take a minute and think about the type of sound you're looking for. (Remember the first commandment of recording drums, back in Chapter 2? *Define Thy Sound.*) Are you in a metal group, looking for that huge, ambient, "drums from hell" sound? Or perhaps you're doing a jazz quartet and you plan on using overheads for your primary mic's to get an authentic acoustic sound, so you want a more moderate, controlled ambience.

Regardless of the type of music you play, keep in mind that unless you're going to use *only* distant room mic's to record your drums (rarely done), the sound on tape won't be as ambient as the actual sound in the room, because the room mic's will be blended (at a relatively low level) with other, closer mic's. This means we're at least as concerned with the *quality* of the ambience as the exact *quantity* of it. If a room sounds nice to you but you think it might be a little too lively, you can pull down the room mic's a little in the mix. You'll still get the ambient quality that drew you to the room in the first place, but at a level that fits your music. On the other hand, if the room is too dry about all you can do is add effects (like digital reverb)—which, as good as they've gotten lately, are still not exactly the same as the real acoustic ambience you get from a great-sounding room.

So what physical conditions are we looking for in a room to get the sound we want? Not knowing what sound you're looking for, I can't describe *your* perfect room, but I can give you some of my own preferences as guidelines, from which we can draw some general conclusions. (Remember, a lot of this is a matter of personal taste!)

My ideal room would be a non-square structure (either a rectangle or a trapezoid). The exact size isn't as important as the shape and surface coverings, but we want to be comfortable—so we'll say a minimum of 500 square feet (though great drum sounds have been recorded in smaller rooms). The ceiling would be of at least moderate height—ten feet or more—and the floor would be hardwood with some carpeted areas (or better yet, movable area rugs for flexibility). The walls would be a mix of wood, plaster, glass, and diffusion materials, and as long as we're at it let's have a nice quiet ventilation/air conditioning system and good lighting. One more thing: *No* sound should leak in from outside.

Conversely, my nightmare room would be a square room with an 8' ceiling, sheetrock on all four walls, wall-to-wall carpet, poor ventilation, poor lighting, and so little acoustic insulation that whenever a truck goes by you have to redo the take. (You may notice an acute resemblance between this description and your basic remodeled garage.)

In general, we're looking for a variety of surfaces so that no one frequency gets overemphasized. A lively room is fine (within reason) as long as the reflections are spread out fairly evenly over the sound spectrum and there are no obvious acoustic flaws like room boom, flutters, or lack of isolation from the outside world. A higher ceiling will add "air" and (just as importantly) keep you from feeling cramped or confined, whereas a low ceiling can sound harsh and splattery because the cymbals don't have room to develop before they reflect back down into the room.

## Creature Comforts

There's another important aspect that has less to do with a room's acoustic ambience than its *ambiance* (pronounced with a snooty French accent). A room's overall vibe can have a big effect on your creativity, and is dependent on several things. One big factor is lighting. From a practical standpoint it's hard to do anything if the lighting's so bad you can't read a chart or lyric sheet, but there's more to it than that. Good lighting pro-

vides adequate illumination without being overbearing, and especially without shining in your eyes. Soft, indirect lighting is best, and it's a bonus if the intensity can be varied to suit the mood. Some musicians seem to work best with the lights dimmed down low.

Another group of factors comes under the heading of climate control. Obviously the room needs to be kept at a comfortable temperature (although you and your guitarist may disagree as to exactly what that is), but just as important is adequate ventilation. Who wants to spend all day in a stuffy room? Along those lines, it really bothers some people to work in a room that smells like smoke (even if no one's currently smoking inside), so take that into consideration if it applies to anyone in your band. (And *never* smoke in the control room, even if it's your studio. It's absolute death on recording equipment.)

Also consider the furnishings and overall style of the room. I'm not going to get into a discussion on interior decorating other than to suggest that you ask yourself the question: "Do I feel comfortable in this room?" This is not a trivial issue. Lots of musicians find it hard to be creative in a "sterile studio atmosphere," which is one of the main reasons given by many recording artists as to why they've started recording at home.

As a final point, don't forget practical amenities. Besides the basics (a clean washroom and a full coffee pot), don't forget things like nearby access to

**A medium-sized commercial studio (like Tom Gingell's Moon Recording) can often be a good compromise between technical potential (space, equipment quality, number of mic's, etc.) and economy.**

food, a quiet place to hang while other folks in your band are finishing their parts, and maybe facilities for a quick snack between takes. Unless you're doing something like a quickie three-song demo, the place you choose is going to be your "home away from home" for quite a while. So try to pick a room where you can work in a relaxed and creative fashion.

## Drumkit Location

Once you've picked a room, where should you set up? Don't assume that just because every other drummer sets up in a certain area that you have to, as well. The "standard spot" may have been picked more for convenience than acoustics, or you may just prefer a different sound than everyone else. Try different areas. Walk around hitting a snare and listening to the room until you find a spot you like.

Also consider the nature of the floor under your kit. It will have a significant effect on your sound because it's the surface closest to your drums. It's good to experiment here, too. My studio has a raised 8' x 12' area with a wood floor for drums. Drummers can either set up directly on the wood, place a small rug down first to help anchor their drums, or cover the entire platform with a carpet prior to setting up. All three configurations yield a different sound. (I once recorded at a studio in L.A. where they had a big piece of polished *sheet metal* set into the floor for the drums. Talk about bright reflections!)

The main point is to be creative. Consider using spaces in the studio not normally used for tracking drums: the foyer, a hallway, a restroom, or even the control room. (Good luck talking the engineer into *that* one.) If the studio's attached to a house, other possibilities open up. For example, the tile bathroom down the hall might be just the thing for that timbale part you're planning to overdub.

## Troubleshooting

Occasionally you'll run into a problem with the acoustics of your recording environment. While you can't remodel the room overnight, there are a few things you can do to improve the situation.

If the room is too live, curtains over some of the walls (especially glass or plaster areas) will cut down on high frequency reflections, as will rugs on hard floors. The addition of furniture (or people, for that matter) will break up reflections, and moving heavy, padded furniture (like sofas or overstuffed chairs) out from the walls a foot or two will form a "bass

trap" and help soak up some excess low end.

A dead room, on the other hand, benefits from the *addition* of hard surfaces. Several years ago, Vinnie Appice described in a *Modern Drummer* interview how he leaned several sheets of plywood together to construct a small, reflective "tent" around his kit in an otherwise dead room. Other options would be to set up next to any reflective surfaces in the studio (such as large windows, mirrors, or sliding glass doors) in an effort to increase reflections. Also remove any rugs, curtains, or diffusion panels from the area if possible, as well as any heavy furniture.

Discrete echoes (flutters or a hard slapback) benefit from the same sort of treatment we applied to a live room. Focus your efforts on the two parallel surfaces (for flutters) or the far wall (for slapbacks).

If you're experiencing too much bleed (not enough isolation between instruments) you can place gobos (small sound-deadening panels) between instruments, if available. Otherwise you can use heavy packing blankets hung over mic' booms to help isolate guitar amps from drums. If the situation becomes intolerable you may wish to consider tracking each instrument individually. (We'll discuss this in detail in chapter 11.)

In a worst-case scenario you may find yourself recording in a room with *horrible* acoustics. (Maybe it's your brother-in-law's studio and he's giving you free time.) In any case, don't give up. Remember our credo: *We can record anywhere.* In this instance what we want to do is take pains to *eliminate* as much of the room sound from the mix as possible. Use no ambient mic's. Pull the overheads down close to the cymbals to reduce the room sound, and roll off the low end on them to further isolate the cymbals. Mike each individual drum as closely as possible to avoid any of the offensive room sound leaking into your tracks. (If you really want to get aggressive about this, use noise gates. See chapter 8 for the lowdown.) During the mix, use a good digital reverb to add ambience back to your tracks. And there you have it: good (if not great) drum tracks from a bad room.

The most important thing about a good room sound—even beyond making your tracks sound good on tape—is that, just like a good drumset, it makes you feel good when you play. This will do more for your music than any piece of technology.

# Resonant Frequencies

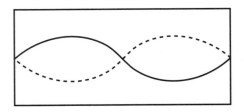

A note whose wavelength equals one dimension of the room will be reinforced.

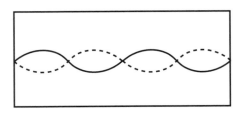

This effect also occurs with notes whose frequencies are multiples of the resonant frequency.

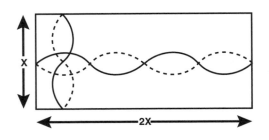

When two or more dimensions of a room are the same or multiples of each other (as in this example), the effect is strengthened and can cause "room boom."

# Acoustic Surface Effects

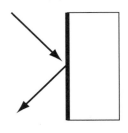

## Reflection

Hard surfaces bounce sound back, creating discrete echoes.

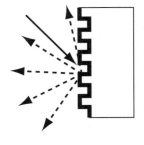

## Diffusion

Variegated surfaces create scattered reflections, yielding ambience without discrete echoes.

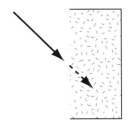

## Absorption

Thick, porous surfaces absorb sound, yielding little or no reflection.

## Acoustics

### Q. What sort of room do you prefer to record in?

**Kenny Aronoff:** I used to be into "the bigger, the better," but now I definitely prefer a medium-sized room where you have a controlled type of ambience. If you're going for the room sound and the room is *too* big, the drums start to lose a little bit of definition. If you have a lot of musicians and a lot of instruments in a big room, that sound really takes up a lot of space on the tape. If it's a power trio, that's different: You *want* to have space in the music—otherwise it starts to clutter up everything.

Each room has a personality: Some are warmer, some are brighter, some are ambient. John Mellencamp's room, for example, is very bright. It's pretty tall but not very wide, and my type of snare drum sound really gets exemplified. Lately I've been trying to play for the room a little bit more. There's a point where you can overplay the room. You play too hard and oversaturate the room with sound, and the drums don't sound as good. I'll tell an engineer to let me know if I'm overplaying the room.

**Gregg Bissonette:** My favorite type of room is one where my drums sound good—where I go into the room and clap my hands and say, "Wow, this is a great room." My favorite room is probably Ocean Way, where we did Joe Satriani's album. I've also done a bunch of movie scores there. Another one of my favorite rooms is a place in Van Nuys called Sound City, where we did the *Siblings* album. Another one's called O'Henry's, in Burbank.

I like to at least have the option of using the room. Right now a tighter drum sound is in style, so I like to get a nice, tight, close-miked sound—but still have the option of using a room that sounds really good when you throw on the mic's that are thirty feet away. If the engineer knows the room and knows how to get what he wants out of it, then you're in business.

**Jim Keltner:** I love big rooms, small rooms—all kinds of rooms. Sometimes you can get a bigger drum sound in a smaller room; that's something that was a revelation to me a few years ago. When people started putting the drums alone in the big room and having the artist and the other musicians off in tiny little rooms, it was kind of the opposite of the way it used to be. I've noticed that a lot of times the sound of the drums is actually better when they're in a smaller, contained room.

**Rod Morgenstein:** I wonder at this point how important the room actually is if you're dealing with someone who, when they close-mike the drums, can get them sounding pretty good. I'm sure you've talked to people who say the room is everything, but then when you stick all these effects on the track, what difference does it make? I've heard quali-

fied people argue both sides of that, so who knows?

It's nice when you can play in a room that has atmosphere. I'd rather not play in a lunch room that's all fluorescent lighting. The vibe is really important, because when you're under the gun you're the only person in whatever room you're in—whether it's a tiny room or a gigantic room. There are faces on the other side of the glass and you can't hear them—but you see their mouths moving. You can get really uptight thinking that they're talking about how *bad* that last performance was, because your mind'll play tricks. I prefer a room that is comfortable, and they can do that by having a soft kind of lighting.

I remember when the Dixie Dreggs recorded the song "Take It Off The Top." To get a big room effect our producer/engineer, Ken Scott, put a microphone in the bathroom outside the studio and left the door to the studio open. The bathroom had a real snappy sound to it and everybody had to be really quiet. That's one of my favorite drum sounds. It's funny that people spend small fortunes building recording studios and using the most sophisticated equipment—and then you find yourself going for an effect by putting a mic' in a bathroom. [laughs]

**Simon Phillips:** I like a room where the kit sounds good naturally. I tend to like natural ambience rather than reaching for the first digital effect you can lay your hands on. If you have a nice big room, then first of all you've got to be able to control the sound so every track doesn't sound like you're in the garage. But if you've got a good room you can put two or three sets of ambient mic's up at different distances from the kit—giving you different pre-delay times. By mixing around with those and playing with some serious compression you can create wonderful natural ambience. If you gate that you can do whatever you want with it, but it's still essentially a natural, pure sound.

As far as location, you've just got to walk around with the drumkit until you find the best place. Or you can do a couple of songs in one part of the room, then move to another part. Most studios, especially in the States, are pretty good about knowing where the drumkit sounds best. They've usually done a lot of experiments. If I didn't know the studio from my own experience, I would tend to go with what they recommend.

It's a funny thing: I've taken a snare, walked around the room hitting it until I said, "This is a good place," and put the kit there. But though it sounded great where I was, when I heard it back in the control room it didn't sound as good as maybe it would have if I had used the place they recommended. One must be careful. If it's a good, well-known studio, then you've got to take the advice of the people who work there every day.

**J.R. Robinson:** I've been in all kinds of situations. I'll give you a couple of examples: I did Steve Winwood's records in

New York City at a studio called Unique. The room was very small—no ambience. I was working with an engineer named Tom Lord-Alge, and just the combination of my drum sound and him bringing up the mic's on the console made the sound huge. When I work with Jeff Lorber he puts me in a tiny room in his house, and the drum sound on the records is *great*. Then again we did a Peter Frampton record at O'Henry's in Hollywood, which is a big room, and Chris Lord-Alge was the engineer on that. Chris's whole thing is a lot of compression and getting great sounds off the direct mic's first—and *then* bringing in certain room mic's for certain songs. The combination creates this mammoth, beautifully clean drum sound.

I like it both ways. I'll go into the rooms at Ocean Way or over at Conway-C or O'Henry's and insist upon using the room. It depends on what kind of music you're playing. Obviously the more room you use, the more distant your drums are. If you're doing a dance-oriented record they usually want the drums right up front in your face, and if you start adding room it tends to distance them out.

# CHAPTER 5

# Microphones

There's one thing you can be certain of when recording acoustic drums and cymbals: No matter *how* you record them—digital or analog, two-track or 48-track—every drum sound you hear in the finished mix will have gone through a microphone. Add to this the facts that different models of mic's have different characteristic sounds and that even the *same* mic' will sound different in various locations, and you can see why microphone selection and placement can greatly affect your drum sound.

Before we talk about which mic' to put where, we should look at a few of the basic design criteria that help determine a mic's sonic personality. There's a practical side to knowing some theory instead of just memorizing model numbers. Let's say you think you'd like to try a specific mic' on your hi-hats, but that one isn't available. Instead of trying to *remember* some other recommended model, you would know to audition other available small-diaphragm condensers—and you'd quickly find the general sound you desire. Along these lines you'll notice that while audio pros each have their own preferences when it comes to drum mic's, there's fairly widespread agreement as to which basic *type* is suitable for any given application.

## Microphone Design

The primary way to differentiate mic's is by their method of operation. Most mic's you'll run into can be categorized as either *dynamics* or *condensers*.

*Dynamic* mic's are also known as "moving coil" mic's. They function just like a speaker, only in reverse: Sound pressure moves a diaphragm, which is connected to a coil. The motion of the coil in proximity to a magnet creates an electrical signal, which gets amplified by the mic' preamp at the mixer, and so on.

Dynamic mic's are generally rugged—able to withstand a certain amount of physical abuse and to operate under high sound pressure levels. (Both are important traits for a mic' to have when placed close to a drum!) Their frequency response is often good, but rarely without peaks and dips. Their ability to reproduce high frequencies and transient information is not as good as that of a condenser—although that situation is improving. New, lighter diaphragms have increased transient response, and the use of new magnetic materials (such as neodymium, used in a number of current models) has resulted in higher output.

*Condenser* mic's, on the other hand, work on capacitance. Sound waves cause the diaphragm (which is one plate of the capacitor) to move with respect to a fixed plate. The signal derived from the change in voltage is increased by a small amplifier in the body of the mic' before being sent to the mixer—which is why condensers need a power supply. So-called "true" condensers usually need 48-volt phantom power (supplied by the console or an outboard power supply) to polarize the capacitor and to power the mic' amp. Some pre-polarized "electret" condensers can function on battery power. In terms of durability, condensers are somewhat more fragile than dynamics. But they feature a flatter, more extended frequency response and better transients due to the lower mass of their moving parts, and they're better at capturing subtle nuances.

Another criterion to keep in mind is *diaphragm size*. As a rule, large-diaphragm mic's have a beefier low end, while mic's with smaller diaphragms can extend further into the high end of the frequency spectrum. However, top-quality large condensers (such as AKGs and Neumanns) excel at all points of the bandwidth.

A third important property of microphones is their *polar pattern*. An *omnidirectional* mic' will pick up sounds evenly from all directions. A mic' with a *cardioid* pattern is directional—it's more responsive to what's in front of it than to sounds coming from behind. A *hypercardioid* is like a cardioid, but more so—it has a tighter pickup pattern with greater off-axis rejection. A *figure-eight* pattern picks up from the front and rear, but not from the sides.

Polar patterns are important because part of controlling your drum sound is controlling isolation—that is, reducing leakage into individual mic's. If you're close-miking a tom and you don't want the cymbal above it to bleed into the tom mic', you'd be far better off with a hypercardioid mic' than with an omnidirectional one, while an omni may be just the thing for capturing the room ambience.

Two other convenient features offered by some mic's are attenuation switches ("pads") and bass roll-off switches. The former allow you to place mic's in high-volume locations (such as near drums) without distortion, while the latter provide a transparent way to remove some bass frequencies from the signal.

## Miking Arrangements

You can radically vary the overall sound of your kit—without changing your drums, your tuning, or the type of mic's you're using—by employing different mic' arrangements. For example, if you're looking for an organic, acoustic rendering of your drums, try a traditional jazz miking setup. Though the details may vary, the concept is to consider the drumset as a single instrument (rather than a group of individual instruments) and mike it accordingly. This usually consists of placing a pair of mic's over the drumset and a mic' in front of the bass drum, and it can result in a very realistic rendering of the drums. (For a stellar example of this, listen to Sheffield Lab's *Drum And Track* audiophile CD. It features a solo drum performance by Jim Keltner, miked in this fashion with absolutely no equalization or processing of any kind. The sound is amazing.)

For more isolation and a punchier, contemporary sound (popular on most types of music outside of jazz and symphonic) you'll probably want to use close miking. This means a mic' on every drum in your kit (and one on the hi-hats, too), along with a pair of overheads for the cymbals. Though this technique takes more time and equipment, it gives you more flexibility and control over your drum sound.

## Selection And Placement

Mic' *selection* is more a matter of personal taste and opinion than an exact science, and a lot of factors apply. Do you want your drums to sound warm, or a little on the bright side? Can you use some bleed, or do you need a tight pattern? With which mic's is the engineer familiar, and which mod-

**Microphone selection and placement make a major contribution to your drum sound.**

els are available?

These last considerations are biggies. Most studios can't afford an unlimited collection of microphones, and you may occasionally have to substitute something else for one of your preferred models. By the same token, the engineer may have a favorite mic' that he's very familiar with and can get good results with. In these instances your best bet is to go with what the studio has and the engineer prefers. After all, in the final analysis your musical skills and the engineer's technical abilities are more important than any single piece of hardware. (The late Larrie Londin once stated in *Modern Drummer* that his favorite recorded drum sound had been achieved by an engineer using nothing but a handful of Shure *SM57s*.)

Mic' *placement* is equally subjective. It's also one of those areas where some experimentation is downright mandatory. Here are some general guidelines to get you started: If you want more lows, move the mic' to within an inch or two of the drumhead. Assuming you're using a directional mic', the proximity effect will boost the bottom end. For more attack, aim the mic' at the place where the stick meets the head. For clarity of tone, back the mic' up a little. For increased ambience (room interaction), back the mic' up a lot. For more "wash" in hi-hats (or individually miked cymbals), aim at the edge of the cymbal; for more brightness/clarity, aim towards the bell. For more beater attack in kick drums, put the mic' well inside the drum, aimed at the beater contact spot. To reduce the attack, aim away from the beater. To add shell resonance, back the mic' off the batter head.

The best (and quickest) way to gain an understanding of mic' placement is to have someone hit one of your drums—with the mic' placed in different locations—while you listen to the results in the control room monitors. If assistance isn't available, record the exercise while moving the mic' yourself and giving verbal cues for the tape ("now the mic' is four inches above the rim, angled toward the center of the head"). Make your decisions after carefully listening to the playback.

The following recommendations come from my own experience and personal preferences, as well as years of picking the brains of other engineers, drummers, producers, and sound techs. Again, these are matters of personal opinion, based on technical or artistic preferences. There is no "right" or "wrong" microphone for any given application.

Whatever gives you the result you envision in your head is the best one for you, so feel free to use whatever works. Hopefully these recommendations will help you on your way.

**Kick.** The consensus here is to use a large-diaphragm dynamic mic', with the AKG *D-112* and *D-12E* and the Sennheiser *MD-421* being popular choices. Also recommended are the Beyer *M-88* and *TGX-50*, the Electro-Voice *RE-20*, the Audio-Technica *ATM25*, and the Shure *SM7* and *Beta 52*. On the other hand, a few artists and engineers swear by the wide frequency range afforded by such condenser mic's as Shure's *SM91* (whose flat base allows it to sit comfortably atop muffling pads) and Applied Microphone Technology's *M-40*. As mentioned earlier, you should experiment with varying the distance between the mic' and the batter head, and with aiming the mic' toward or away from the beater.

Some engineers employ a two-mic' technique, with a fairly aggressive dynamic mic' (like the Sennheiser *421*) near the beater-contact spot, and a large, warm condenser (usually a Neumann *U-47*) a ways back from the front of the drum to get some "air." The two signals are mixed until the right balance of attack and resonance is achieved.

**Snare**. A dynamic, vocal-type mic' is the preference here. The majority of drummers and engineers give the nod to the venerable Shure *SM57*, for good reason. Its non-linear frequency response happily corresponds with what most of us want to hear in a snare—even over other, supposedly "better" mic's. They can also take high volume levels without giving up the ghost. (Recently I decided to audition three mic's on a very nice maple snare I was preparing to record. I put up a *57*, a more expensive dynamic, and a top-flight, "studio-quality" large-diaphragm condenser. I ended up going with the *57*.) Other mic's with similar qualities include Shure's *SM58* as well as their *Beta 57* and *Beta 58*, the Electro-Voice *N/Dym* series of vocal mic's, the Audix *D-series*, and just about any of the better vocal dynamics from Beyer, AKG, or Sennheiser. Occasionally, folks will run a small-diaphragm condenser on a snare to increase crispness, or will run an additional mic' (usually a small condenser) *under* the snare, for the same reason. (Whenever you mic' both sides of a drum, try throwing the bottom mic' out of polarity from the top one. This may improve the sound.) When miking the snare, a good place to start is with the mic' above the rim looking down towards the head at an angle, with the diaphragm a couple of inches off the head.

**Toms**. Medium and large dynamics are the favored types here, with a couple of exceptions. Sennheiser's *421* gets a lot of use, as does their *409*. So does the good old *SM57*. Electro-Voice's *N/D 308* and *N/D 408* also have fans due to their nice sound and relatively small size, and the flexibility of their pivoting yoke. The newer Sennheiser *MD-504* sounds great and is quite small, as is the Audix *D-2*, whose size belies its fat sound. Also of interest is Shure's new *Beta 56*, which is small and features a built-in pivot. Some engineers rely on expensive large condensers (notably the Neumann *U-87*) for the gorgeous sound they produce, while some drummers are going the other way with very small clip-on condensers like the AKG *C408*, the Shure *SM98*, the Audio-Technica *ATM35*, the K&K *CTM-3*, and the Applied Microphone Technology *A-95*. These little mic's have good transient response, and they pick up the fundamental note of the drum well due to close positioning. They also stay out of the way and don't require a forest of boom stands to support them. Mic' placement on toms is similar to the recommended technique for snares. Be sure to experiment with varying the miking distance—when using mic's close to drums, half an inch either way can make a noticeable difference.

**Hi-Hats**. Small-diaphragm condensers fit this job description to a "T." Their very quick transient response and smooth extension into the highest frequencies give clear, sparkling highs, while an absence of beef in the bottom octaves is actually an asset for this application. Preferred models include the Neumann *KM-84* and *KM-184* and AKG's *451*, *452*, and *460*, as well as the Shure *SM81*, Audio-Technica's *4031* and *4051*, and the *SCX-1* from Audix. Start with the mic' four to eight inches above the top cymbal, pointing down at an angle. Play around with aiming at the bell, the edge, and the stick contact spot. Also, experiment with placing the mic' so that it doesn't get a lot of bleed from the rest of the kit (especially the snare).

**Overheads**. The big decision here is whether you're using overheads to pick up the entire kit or just the cymbals. If you're primarily after cymbals, use a small-diaphragm condenser similar to the type recommended for hi-hats. To accurately reproduce the whole drumset, most engineers choose large-diaphragm condensers. The most cherished mic' for this application is the classic tube microphone from

AKG, the *C12*, but at $12,000 a pair (used) you're unlikely to find them outside of major studios. The Neumann *U-87* is also quite popular, as is AKG's *414*. One of my current favorites for the job is AKG's new "vintage" *414B TLII*, which was specifically designed to sound like the *C12*, but at about a quarter the cost. Audio-Technica's *AT 4033* and *AT 4050* and Neumann's *TLM-193* are also good choices (as is almost any studio-quality large condenser).

## Coincident Pair (XY) Miking

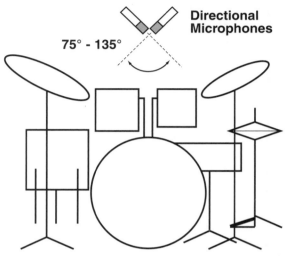

This arrangement yields a natural stereo image with no phase problems because all sounds arrive at each microphone simultaneously.

## Spaced Pair (AB) Miking

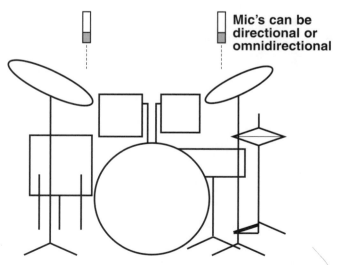

This arrangement gives good separation and strong stereo imaging. Check for phase problems by summing to mono.

Probably the easiest placement technique for overheads is the *XY* position (diaphragms almost touching at a 75° to 135° angle). This gives you good stereo imaging with no attendant phase problems. You may also wish to try hanging the mic's in a "spaced pair" configuration several feet apart over the kit for more separation. If you do, check for phase problems by listening for a thin, hollow character to the sound when both mic's are up in the mix. If this happens, move one of the mic's a little at a time until the situation improves.

## Phase Cancellation

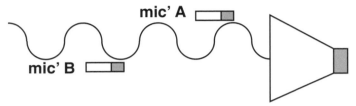

Microphones A and B are picking up the signal 180° out of phase from each other. Possible solutions are to move one of the mic's until proper phase is restored, or to reverse polarity on either of the mic's.

**Ambient Mic's.** If you're tracking in a nice-sounding room, it never hurts to put up a couple (or more) microphones to capture some of the ambience. Most folks prefer large condensers for this task (the same as for overheads). Some use them in the omni mode to get the entire room, while others use cardioid patterns to control what they're picking up. One engineer told me that he uses a cardioid pattern with the mic' aimed *toward* the wall, to get more reflections. In this situation, placement is up to your discretion; there are no pat answers. Your best bet is to walk around the room—listening for that magic spot where your drums sound the way you hear them in your head—and then to place the mic's accordingly.

## Recommended Overhead/ Ambient/Room Microphones

AKG 414B TLII

Audio-Technica
AT 4050

Audio-Technica
AT 4033

Neumann TLM-193

# Recommended Kick Drum Microphones

Sennheiser MD-421

AKG D-112

Electro-Voice RE-20

Beyer TGX-50

Shure Beta 52

Shure SM7

Applied Microphone Technology M-40

Beyer M-88

Audio-Technica ATM25

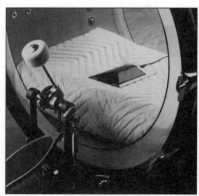

Shure SM91

# Recommended Tom Microphones

Sennheiser MD-409

Electro-Voice N/D 408

Sennheiser MD-504

Audix D2

Shure Beta 56

Neumann U-87

AKG C419 (top) and C418
(upgrades of C408 model)

Shure SM98

Audio-Technica ATM35

K&K CTM3

Applied Microphone Technology A-95

# Recommended Snare Drum Microphones

Audix D1

Shure SM57

Shure Beta 57

Electro-Voice N/D 308

# Recommended Hi-Hat Microphones

Neumann KM-184

AKG 460

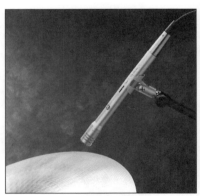
Shure SM81

Audio-Technica 4031

Audio-Technica 4051

Audix SCX-1

## Drum Microphones

**Q. Are there certain mic's that you prefer on your drums because of the way they sound?**

**Kenny Aronoff:** The mic's I want on my drums are the mic's that make me sound good. [laughs] Mic's that sound great in one room can sound completely different in another room. The whole thing about mic's is the engineer and what he does with them. Contributing factors in the way a mic' sounds are the outboard gear, the way the mic' is EQ'd, and the room.

I'm still a big fan of the Shure SM57 on the snare. On the bass drum I tend to like two mic's: I like a mic' with a lot of aggression, like the Sennheiser 421. But it's a little bright, so we have to put another mic' in there to get a meatier sound—maybe an old tube mic' or occasionally the AKG D-12E. On the toms I use the 421, the Shure 57, the AKG C408 clip-ons, and the Shure SM98s.

**Gregg Bissonette:** I've heard guys walk in and say, "Man, you've got to put Sennheiser 421s on all my toms, a 57 on my snare, and I want to use that PZM mic' on my bass drum with a D-112...." What right do you have doing that? It's like them telling you what kind of sticks to use. If they can get a great sound with all 57s on the drums, at least give them a chance. If the sound isn't happening, then you might make some suggestions. But the last thing anybody wants is to be told what to do.

Having said that, I do have some personal favorites. On toms I really like the Sennheiser 421s, and for the bass drum I've had good luck with the same, or an AKG D-112. I also like the Shure SM91 on the bass drum. On the snare, just a 57. For overheads I like the AKG 414s a lot.

**Jim Keltner:** I use a microphone in my bass drum that I really believe is fantastic—an AKG D-112. A lot of guys are using it now. I have both heads on my bass drum, so what they'll do is take a Neumann U47 or something and put it on the outside.

**Simon Phillips:** I supply the kit with bass drum mic's because the bass drums have front heads on. The mic's are already inside and wired up. I'm using AKG D-12s—the older ones. On the toms I use Electro-Voice ND 308s. I supply those because most studios don't have six identical mic's with the same age and same usage on them, so they might sound a bit different. But as for all the other mic's, I like SM57s for the snare drums—everybody's got those. Everybody's got some condenser mic's for the hi-hats and the overheads, and pretty much everybody has an M-88 or an RE-20 or a U47. So I don't bother about those mic's.

**J.R. Robinson:** On the kick drum I'll use a Shure SM91 or Beta 52. I've also had good luck with the Audio-Technica ATM25. On the snare drum I use the old standby Shure SM57 and maybe an AKG 452 on the bottom. On the hi-hat, usually it's a 452 or a Neumann KM84. But I've been in situations in those little home studios where all they have are 57s, and I'll tell you what: You can put a Shure SM57 on anything and EQ it and it'll sound good. They're very dependable microphones for getting sounds quickly.

For overhead mic's I really like the AKG C12s. If God ever made a microphone it was this one. [laughs] If you just put them over the kit, you get a beautiful warm sound. The AKG 414 is also a great overhead mic'.

**Q. From an engineer's perspective, what are your favorite drum mic's?**

**Mike Fraser:** On the kick, a Sennheiser 421 or an AKG D-12. For the snare, an AKG 414 or a Shure SM57 (or both) on the top, and a 57 on the bottom. On toms sometimes I use Neumann U87s, but a lot of studios don't have that many of them, so I'll rely on 57s. For more attack I'll go to Sennheiser 421s. If we want a brash sound from the hi-hats I'll use a Neumann KM-84. If it needs a more expansive sound, I'll put up an AKG 451. For overheads I'll use any great tube mic's that they've got around, and for room sound I'll generally just throw up a couple of Neumann U87s.

**Ed Thacker:** I like an AKG D-112 or a Sennheiser 421 for up close in a kick. Then I'll add a Neumann U47 for back a ways. On snares I reach for the ol' 57, an AKG 452, or a Neumann KM-84. On toms I'll use Sennheiser 421s top and bottom and out of phase with each other. For hi-hats I occasionally use a Beyer 160, but usually the AKG 451. I like AKG C-12s for overheads if the studio has them. My choice for room sound varies, but usually I'll use the U87s in cardioid, facing away from the drums.

# CHAPTER 6

# Equalization

Equalization is simply the amplification or attenuation of selected frequencies (rather than the whole bandwidth). Every time we turn up the treble on our stereo we're applying EQ. As basic as this process seems, EQ can have a tremendous impact on the sound of your drums. So it's worthy of a little investigation.

## Different Types Of EQ

Types of equalizers commonly found in studios include: graphic equalizers, fixed-point shelving equalizers, and semi-parametric and parametric equalizers, along with enhancers. *Graphics* have a number of sliders controlling different frequencies—usually in one-octave (10-band), 2/3-octave (15-band) or 1/3-octave (30-band) intervals. The advantages are that you can boost or cut several frequency points at once, and you can see the resulting response curve with a glance at the sliders (hence the name "graphic" equalizer). The disadvantages are that you can only control a fixed set of frequencies (indicated on the sliders), and your signal is going through from ten to thirty amplifiers, which can add distortions to the signal. *Parametrics* allow you to choose the frequency being boosted or cut, the bandwidth on either side of the center point (a steep notch or a broad curve), and the amount of boost or cut. These are useful for problem situations—like notching out a specific unpleasant overtone—and are usually outboard devices (though some high-end boards incorporate fully parametric EQ on each channel).

Much more common are semi-parametric and shelving EQs, which are found on most boards. You should familiarize yourself with their operation, because they will be front-line tools for shaping the sound of your drums. Typically each input channel of a board will have shelving EQ for the lows and highs, with one or two bands of semi-parametric EQ for the mids.

*Shelving* EQ means that everything below or above a fixed point (such as 100 Hz for the low end and 10 kHz for the

The Alesis M-EQ 230 is a two-channel graphic equalizer.

The Rane PE 17 is a five-band parametric equalizer.

highs) is amplified or attenuated equally. This means that when you boost the highs (for example), you're not just creating a peak centered at 10 kHz. Instead you are actually boosting everything from 10 kHz on up to the limits of the system (probably 18-20 kHz), creating a response curve that looks like a shelf. Sometimes the shelf points are switchable, allowing you to choose between two frequencies for the low end (for example: 60 or 120 Hz) and two for the highs (6 or 12 kHz). If this is the case, you should definitely try both points when tweaking your drum sounds, because they each produce results with a different character.

*Semi-parametric* equalizers (frequently called "sweepable mids" when used to control midrange on the board EQ) are just like their fully parametric big brothers, except that they have no control for widening or narrowing the bandwidth around the selected frequency. This makes for simpler operation: You set the amount of boost or cut, then "sweep" the spectrum until you find the appropriate frequency.

*Enhancers*, along with similar processors known as *exciters*, are devices that add sheen to the high end (by phase realignment and program-dependent EQ). Many current models also have provisions for beefing up the low end. They're usually used on an entire mix rather than on a single instrument (though I'll occasionally use one to brighten a snare). However, they can come in handy if all your drums (on the multitrack tape) sound a little dull. You could send your entire drum mix (via a stereo sub-mix) through an enhancer, which can do a lot to revitalize your sound.

## Know Your Drum

One of the best ways to maintain control of your drum sound in a recording environment is to get to know the frequency spectrum of your drum. Any good equalizer (parametric or graphic, as long as individual frequencies are clearly marked) can be used to analyze specific regions of a drum. To do this, run your drum signal (either live off the mic' or from a tape) through the equalizer. First boost and then cut at each of several frequencies, starting from the low end and working your way up. Listen critically to the results. We're looking for those "sweet spots," where a subtle boost may enhance a warm fundamental, or perhaps sharpen the crack of a snare. We're also looking for "sour spots," where reducing certain frequencies will eliminate unmusical

tones and improve the overall timbre of the drum. *Make notes* regarding the results of this exercise; they'll save you time and frustration once you're in the studio and the clock is running.

## Sweet & Sour Snare, To Go

Enough theory; let's get down to nuts and bolts. Since the snare drum produces the most complex sound and is probably the most important in defining a "signature" sound, we'll use it for the bulk of our examples. I ran the above exercise using what I thought was a good "middle ground" drum/mic' combination: a 5x14 chrome snare (with a coated *Ambassador* head tuned medium-tight) with a Shure *SM57* over the drum at an angle, two inches off the top head. A 31-band graphic and four bands of parametric EQ were utilized for the sake of reporting accurate results. However, in the real world I almost always use just the onboard EQ. It's clean and quiet, and it can get a musical sound very quickly.

You should be aware that different drums (or similar drums with different heads or tuning) will favor other frequencies, as will different mic's. So although my test results will get you in the ballpark, you will definitely benefit from running this exercise with *your* drums. That said, let's look at what we've got.

Our test snare put out absolutely nothing below 50 Hz, and nothing musical below 80 Hz. The "meat" of the drum resides between 125 and 250 Hz, centered at 200 Hz. Pulling this down thinned out the drum and made the snare wires more prominent, while boosting it fattened up the drum (more on this piccolo/fatback thing in a moment).

There was a little head ring at 500 Hz. You could leave it in for a "live" sound or reduce it to dry out the drum a little. Between 800 and 1,200 Hz we get the "stick on head" sound. Too much here can sound "papery" or "flappy." (Hold an unmounted head in your hand and whack it with a stick. *That's* the sound I'm talking about.) In the 2,500 to 3,150 Hz region there was some midrange harshness that wasn't too musical. Realistically we can take care of all three of these situations with a broad, gentle midrange reduction using onboard sweepable midrange EQ: Set the gain for a mild reduction (-3 dB) and sweep the frequency control back and forth until things smooth out a little. Be careful— too much "mid suck-out" will take all the bite out of your sound.

Enhancers (like this BBE 862 Sonic Maximizer) add sheen to the high end of a signal.

At the top end, a little boost between 6.3 and 8 kHz brought out the crack of the drum, but too much here can be annoying. The sound of the snare wires can be brought out (or buried) by an adjustment up at 12.5 kHz, and above that there's only "air"—those subtle little transients that aren't really noticeable but add life to a track.

## Three In One

Perhaps you want the sound of a deep snare or a piccolo for a certain song, but you only have a regular snare with you. All is not lost. I got a nice fat-back sound by boosting the frequencies from 200 Hz (the "meat") down to 80 Hz (the lowest useful overtone) and cutting both the head ring and the "papery" sound with a broad reduction centered at 800 Hz. A little dip between 3 and 4 kHz smoothed it out a little, while a slight increase at 12.5 kHz helped maintain the "snariness."

A reasonable facsimile of a piccolo snare could be had by rolling off from 100 to 200 Hz to thin it out, adding a *tiny* bit at 315 to 400 Hz to add a little ringing "thonk" for liveness, and boosting everything above 12 kHz a little for crispness.

## Other Drums

The same sort of analysis on a 12" tom revealed a nice, warm "boom" when a boost was applied at 125 Hz (that was the meat of this particular drum), a "bong" at 500 Hz that I reduced slightly, and a sour "wang" overtone (okay—probably the result of imperfect tuning) at 1,600 that I notched out. A little boost between 5 and 8 kHz (centered at 6.3 kHz) added some attack, and that was that: a nice, fat tom sound with plenty of articulation.

A 24" bass drum had nothing useful below 40 Hz. At 60 to 80 Hz there was a fundamental that really boomed if I cranked it up, (Apply this sparingly if at all.) There were some ugly low-mid overtones from 400 to 800 Hz (particularly at 700 Hz) that I pulled back a little. A shelving EQ boosted everything above 6 kHz a little to add some beater attack.

With cymbals there is nothing useful below 120 Hz (and with the right mic', a low-end roll-off is usually all you need to do). The "cut" of cymbals and hi-hats resides at around 6 kHz, and "sparkle" can be added with a 12 kHz shelf. But be careful with these high-end boosts; too much will sound harsh and will quickly fatigue the listener.

## Guiding Principles

Although EQ can be used as a special effect (like making your 5" snare sound like an 8" snare), it's generally used in a "corrective" mode to make your drums on tape exhibit more of the same qualities you love about live drums.

Think of recording your drums as analogous to photographing an attractive model for the cover of a glamour magazine, with EQ as part of the cosmetics package (make-up and hair style). We don't want to make the model look like someone other than who she really is; we just want to enhance her natural beauty. The same goes for your drums. Certain aspects of the recording process can diminish *their* natural beauty, but the judicious use of equalization can help restore those qualities so they can shine in their best light.

# Drum Frequency Analysis

This chart indicates where various sonic characteristics were found on the test drum.* Other drums will have similar characteristics, but those characteristics may be located at different frequencies.

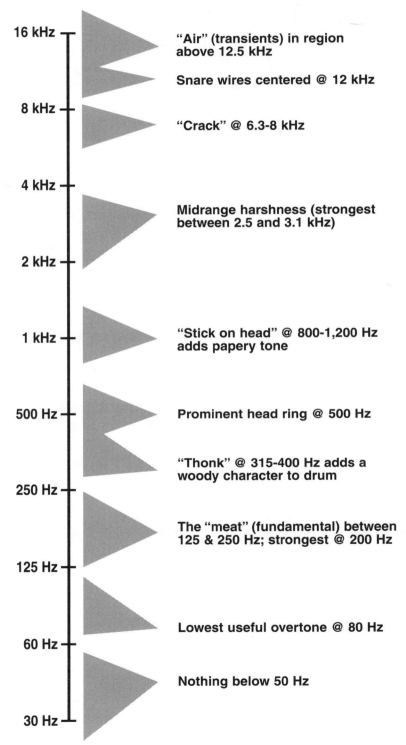

16 kHz — "Air" (transients) in region above 12.5 kHz

Snare wires centered @ 12 kHz

8 kHz — "Crack" @ 6.3-8 kHz

4 kHz — Midrange harshness (strongest between 2.5 and 3.1 kHz)

2 kHz —

1 kHz — "Stick on head" @ 800-1,200 Hz adds papery tone

500 Hz — Prominent head ring @ 500 Hz

"Thonk" @ 315-400 Hz adds a woody character to drum

250 Hz — The "meat" (fundamental) between 125 & 250 Hz; strongest @ 200 Hz

125 Hz —

Lowest useful overtone @ 80 Hz

60 Hz — Nothing below 50 Hz

30 Hz —

*Test drum: 1966 Ludwig *Supraphonic* (5x14) w/coated *Ambassador* batter head & *Ambassador* snare-side head (both tensioned medium-tight).

# CHAPTER 7

# Compression

Whether you're aware of it or not, most popular recordings have some dynamic compression applied to them in one form or another. (In fact, one of the attributes of properly applied compression—in this context—is that it's *not* readily apparent). That said, compression can do lots of beneficial things for the sound of your drums—some subtle and some dramatic. But before we get into that, let's briefly talk about what compressors are and how they work.

## Compressors At Work

A compressor is a device used to reduce the dynamic range of a signal by a given amount once the signal exceeds a specific level. The "given amount" is called the *compression ratio*, and the "specific level" is called the *threshold*. They work in tandem (along with a couple of other variables) like this: Let's say you set a compressor for a ratio of 2:1 with a threshold of 0 dB. Then you send a drum signal through it (either while tracking or

from tape). As long as you're playing at a moderate volume and the signal level is below the threshold, the compressor will pass it along unimpeded. Now let's suppose you really slam the drum, sending a +6 dB spike to the compressor. The compressor will reduce the peak to +3 dB (cutting it in half, your 2:1 ratio) before sending the drum signal to the next step in the recording chain. Once the peak is over, the compressor quits the gain reduction act and things are as they were prior to the above-threshold signal.

## Attack & Release

You'd think a processor would have to be pretty quick to catch and reduce a snare hit in real time, and you'd be right. In fact, the "other variables" mentioned above relate to exactly that: how fast the compressor clamps down on an incoming peak and how quickly it lets up afterwards. These features are known respectively as the *attack* and *release* times. A normal range of attack times might

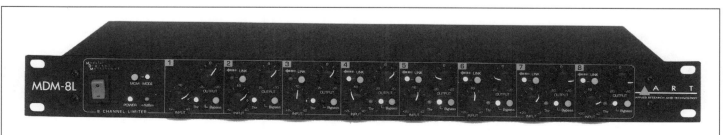

The ART MDM-8L eight-channel limiter is a single-function processor.

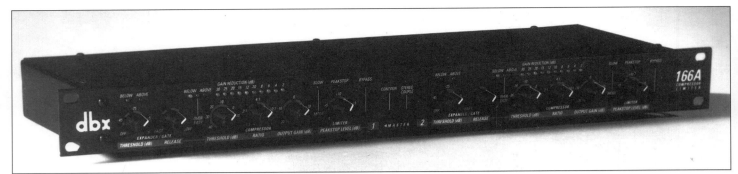

Compressors tend to be multi-function processors, like this dbx 166A compressor/limiter...

run from less than a millisecond to 50 milliseconds, while release times are typically from 100 milliseconds to several seconds. For most percussion applications you generally want fast attack and release times (for obvious reasons), while more legato parts like cymbal swells or entire mixes usually sound more musical with slower attack and release times.

Many compressors today have program-dependent automatic attack and release, which means that they adjust the parameters of these controls according to the incoming material. A signal with quick transients (like most drum signals) will generate quicker times than a slow bass guitar part, for example. Most compressors with auto attack and release (such as the ubiquitous dbx *160* series) are very user-friendly and transparent in use, allowing you to get a musical sound in short order.

## Knees & Limits

Classic compression works as described earlier: Signals under threshold are unprocessed, and anything over threshold is fully compressed at the given ratio. This is known as *hard knee* compression because a graph of the signal output has a hard bend (knee) at the threshold, where compression starts. *Soft knee* compression, on the other hand, comes on a little more gradually. Signals near the threshold are compressed at less than the full ratio, with compression increasing the further the

input gain exceeds the threshold until the full ratio is reached. This "variable ratio" type of compression is somewhat smoother and less noticeable in use—which may or may not be to your liking depending on whether you're looking for a natural-sounding reduction or a more dynamic effect. (More about this in a minute.)

A device closely related to the compressor is the *limiter*. Briefly stated, a limiter is a compressor with such a high ratio that the signal virtually *can't* exceed the threshold. (From a practical standpoint, any compressor set above 10:1 is going to function as a limiter.) Limiters are used when you absolutely don't want a signal to go beyond a certain level, for any number of reasons.

## Why Compress/Limit?

There are an infinite number of applications where compressors or limiters are useful, but almost all of them fit into one of three categories. One reason to compress is a purely technical one: to keep from overdriving the recording equipment.

Compared to other instruments, drums have a large dynamic range, capable of going from very subtle to extremely loud in a split second. These high-level transients can overload recorders if the peaks are too hot, leading to distortion. Why not simply turn the signal down? You could, of course, but that might lower the level of the quiet parts to the point where they get lost in the mix.

Compression, on the other hand, will just reduce

...this dbx 266 compressor/gate...

...this dbx 1066 compressor/limiter/gate...

the peaks, allowing the more subtle stuff to be heard. This is known as getting the signal to "fit" onto the tape. All recorders, whether analog or digital, have a finite dynamic range with a noise floor at the bottom and distortion at the top. The hotter the signal you can send to tape (without creating distortion), the better your signal-to-noise ratio is going to be. (And while overdriving a digital recorder leads to absolutely unusable digital distortion, slightly oversaturated analog tape produces a warm, musical compression of its own, which is why some pros prefer analog machines over digital for cutting punchy rhythm tracks.)

Another reason to compress is to smooth out uneven dynamics. Let's say you've recorded a great backing track with your rhythm section, but during the mix you notice that at some points the kick drum is played a little harder than at others. You have the option of redoing the entire track, but that's time-consuming and expensive. (Besides—it was a great take, remember?) A practical solution is to slightly compress the kick track, allowing you to bring the overall level up to where the weaker hits are hot enough to drive the groove but the peaks don't stick out too much. Bass guitar is frequently compressed for the same reason, and a properly compressed kick track and bass guitar track can work together to give your recordings a solid, tight bottom that's not booming out of control.

The third and best reason to compress drums doesn't have as much to do with gain or dynamics as it does with *sound*. Part of the magic of compression is that it can make things sound "loud" without increasing the actual level. It works like this: A hard-hit snare has a totally different sound quality than a lightly hit one, *even disregarding the obvious difference in volume*. The one you slammed has more overtones ("punch," "ring," "bite," etc.) than the one you tapped, and it's these overtones that give the human ear clues as to the loudness of the original source material—regardless of the playback volume. Compression raises the level of these overtones relative to the rest of the drum sound. And because it takes a certain amount of time (albeit small) to clamp down on the signal, the stick attack cuts through clearly. Add to this the fact that compression also *increases* sustain (because as the sound decays the compressor "lets up," raising the level of the sustain relative to the peak of the note), and you've got a recipe for a big, fat, aggressive drum sound that will still fit into the dynamic range of your chosen recording medium.

## Applications

One of the first things to consider when using a compressor is how to avoid noise buildup. (When you raise the average level you're also raising the noise floor.) There are several things you can do in this regard.

First, *keep your levels hot* at every step of the process. Play solidly, close-mike the drums (if appropriate), keep the input levels on the board up, and send a strong signal to tape. Next, *keep acoustic noise reduced to a minimum*. If there's noise in the background, you'll hear it come up

...and this Alesis 3630 compressor/limiter/gate.

when the compressor lets up. This is called "breathing." Avoid it by keeping all extemporaneous noises out when recording. If all else fails, *gate the signal.* Many compressors include a built-in noise gate for just this purpose, but you have to be careful or you'll end up gating out some drum parts along with the unwanted noise. (We'll cover gates in depth in the next chapter.)

Also think about *where* (in the recording chain) to apply compression. You can use it while tracking or while mixing (or a little of both), and there are pros and cons to each option. If you're pretty certain about the sound you're looking for, go ahead and compress while recording the individual tracks. This will help the noise situation a little (you'll avoid boosting any tape noise) and it'll free up another compressor for mixdown. (Compressors—unlike reverbs—are serial processors, meaning that the entire signal passes through them. This, in turn, requires a separate channel of compression for each track requiring individual processing.)

Saving drum compression until the mix is great *if* you're using a quiet multitrack system (like a digital or an open-reel analog with noise reduction), and *if* a number of compressors are available. It gives you the flexibility of trying different compression schemes against the entire mix before committing to one.

What parts of the drumkit should you compress? Good question. Since all of us have slightly different playing styles, there is no absolute answer. But I can certainly give you some general guidelines. The two examples given previously might be a good place to start. Listen to the kick track and see if a little compression doesn't tighten it up, both in terms of tone and dynamics. One of the hallmarks of a contemporary recording (especially in the dance, R&B, and rock genres) is a punchy, tight, *consistent* bottom end, and a compressor can help you achieve it.

As indicated, compression can really help toughen up your snare sound. (It's especially useful for those of you working in the more aggressive end of things.) You may want to experiment with more compression on the snare than you put on the kick.

Some folks like to compress the toms and some don't; it's a matter of taste. You can compress either the close mic's on the toms or the overhead mic's. Doing the latter will also affect the cymbals—especially the crashes. This can be helpful if your cymbals are splattering all over the tape.

If you're recording in a nice-sounding room, you can bring out some of the "air" in the studio by compressing the room mic's. This will let more room ambience in when the compressors let up, adding some live reverberation to the sound.

So how do you dial in the "right" sound? It's mostly trial and error, but there's a logical process that'll make things go smoother. Set the attack and release times (if they're not automatic) close to where you think they should be (faster for kick, snare, or toms; slower for overheads and room mic's). Set a moderate ratio (2:1 or 3:1) if you're just trying to smooth out your dynamics; use a higher one (from 4:1 to 10:1) if you're trying to really change the tonal character. Feed your drum signal through the compressor and slowly start lowering the threshold setting, while listening carefully. Assuming that the other controls are at least in the ballpark, the threshold knob has the most obvious effect on your sound because it determines *how much* of the signal is getting squashed.

Watching the gain-reduction meter will also help at this stage. It'll quickly let you know if you're just smoothing out the occasional peak or compressing the entire part. Once the threshold is set, fine-tune the attack, release, and ratio (if necessary). The important thing here is to use your ears. If it sounds (and feels) good, go with it. Finally, turn up the output control (sometimes called "makeup gain") to make up for the level you lost during the compression stage. Remember, we want to send as hot a signal as possible (short of distortion) to tape.

Once you start applying compression to your drums, you'll find it's a natural process that's not half as complicated as it sounds. While over-processing can (as always) lead to detrimental results, I think you'll find that a little compression can help your recordings sound fuller, tighter, and more consistent.

# Compressor Function

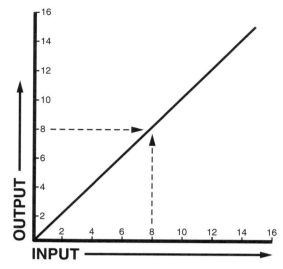

A transfer function chart shows that with no dynamic compression applied, the output is equal to the input (that is, an 8 dB increase in the input signal will yield an 8 dB increase in the output).

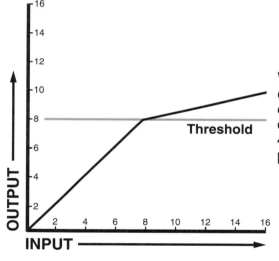

With classic (hard knee) compression applied, the output is equal to the input as long as the input level is below the threshold. Above the threshold, the output equals a specified fraction of the input as determined by the ratio. For example: At a ratio of 4:1, an input increase of 8 dB above the threshold yields an output increase of 2 dB.

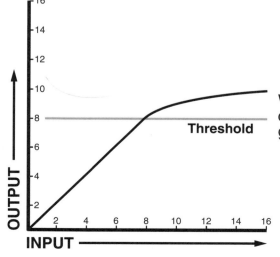

With soft knee compression, signals near the threshold are compressed at less than the full ratio, with the compression gradually increasing as the input level rises.

# CHAPTER 8

# Noise Gates

If any piece of processing gear can be said to be controversial, the noise gate wins the title hands down. No other device engenders such strong feelings among studio drummers (almost like drum machines did during the '80s) and yet is used at almost every studio. Here are some quips from pros we broached the subject with.

**Simon Phillips:** "Absolutely no gates [while tracking]. Leave that for when you mix. And when I mix, I'll *only* use gates on the echo sends to clean up certain things."

**J.R. Robinson:** "I *hate* gates...gating is like playing without your feet and hands—just your arms down to your wrist."

**Kenny Aronoff:** "I tend to prefer stuff that sounds natural. But I have to say that I'll go with whatever it takes to make it sound good."

**Gregg Bissonette:** "I'm not a real big fan of gating the drums, because when you gate them the little grace notes and ghost strokes can get lost."

**Jim Keltner:** "I prefer no gates on my drums. I hate the *concept* of a gate...the shutting down of an instrument. It's stupid."

**Rod Morgenstein:** "I totally understand the importance of gates, and I don't really mind them on the tom-toms. But there must absolutely be no gate on the snare drum, because I'm a ghost-stroke player. When a gate is put on the snare all you're going to hear is the *2* and *4*."

If gates are held in such low regard by many studio pros, why bother to learn about them? And why do so many engineers rely on them for getting drum sounds? Well, part of the answer to the first question actually lies in the second one: If gates *are* used in many studios, you'd better have an understanding of them, if only to be aware of potential problems. (If someone's overgating your snare and starting to lose ghost notes, for example, you'd want to immediately recognize it and possibly offer some suggestions as to how to correct it.)

The rest of the answer is that noise gates *can* be very beneficial under certain circumstances, when applied correctly. First, let's check out some basic theory on how they work.

## Music In—Noise Out

Probably the best way to understand the function of a noise gate is to envision a *real* gate, like Mister

**Noise gates include the dbx 363X Dual Gate...**

...the dbx 172 twin-channel Super Gate...

McGregor might use to keep Peter Rabbit out of his garden. Now imagine that this gate has a hefty spring on it, such that while Old Man McGregor could easily open it and go inside, there's no way little Peter could push it open and make a meal out of his carrot crop. If you consider Mr. McGregor (the desired element) to be *music* and Peter Rabbit (the undesired element) to be *noise*, with the spring-loaded garden gate (the determining factor as to who gets in or not) as the *noise gate*, then you've got a fair picture of the scenario.

Noise gates are configured quite a bit like compressors. They even share some of the same parameters, such as *threshold*, *attack*, and *release*. Their operation is also similar, although the end results are almost opposite: a compressor reduces your dynamic range by lowering the loud parts, while a gate increases the dynamic range by lowering (or eliminating entirely) the quiet parts.

Let's suppose you have a signal containing sounds that you want (a close-miked snare, for example) and other sounds you *don't* want (other drums leaking into the track, or bleed from your guitarist's amp). We can send the signal through a gate and adjust the threshold (the "spring strength," as it were) so that the gate opens up for the snare hits but not for the other noises. This will result in a processed track containing only the snare hits, with no noise in between them. Obviously, for this to work, the "music" must be louder than the "noise," since the gate doesn't really know what we want or don't want. It simply switches on (opens) when it detects a signal above a certain level (the threshold) and switches off (closes) when the signal drops below that level.

Besides the threshold, another important factor is how fast the gate opens once it's triggered. This is the *attack* time, and it may vary from *very* fast (on the order of 50 *micro*seconds or less) to 50 milliseconds or so. How quickly the gate closes is the *release* time, typically ranging from 50 milliseconds up to several seconds. For quick, percussive sounds you usually want the fastest attack possible, in order to make sure you don't chop off the leading

edge of the sound. (These transients are an important part of a drum's character.) With slower sounds it may sound unnatural if the gate pops open all at once, so a slightly longer attack time may be in order. Release times are dependent not only on how quickly the note itself ends but on how much (if any) of the room decay you wish to include. Another important consideration here is how soon the desired note is followed by an undesired one. If you're gating a quarter-note hi-hat part out of a snare track, you can afford quite a long release time.

## Potential Problems

Sounds great so far, right? So why do some folks have a thing against gates? Well, in their quest for sonic perfection certain producers and engineers have gotten overzealous, and have thrown out the baby with the bath water. They get so concerned with eliminating *all* stray noise from a track that they end up also losing some of the subtle intricacies of the part, such as the snare ghost strokes already mentioned.

An opposite problem can also occur, where instead of losing parts you can have the threshold too low and stray parts can leak in, with decidedly unmusical results. Let's say the engineer is gating your snare because he's sending it to a reverb, and he doesn't want reverb on the rest of the kit. So far so good. But if he doesn't take certain precautions (which we'll discuss later) there's a good chance that other loud parts—such as a strong tom stroke or a cymbal crash—can exceed the threshold and make it through the gate. This, in turn, can result in a loud tom or cymbal unexpectedly popping into the mix...with reverb unintentionally splattered all over it!

Incorrect attack and release times can also cause trouble. We already mentioned the problem of having too fast or slow an *attack* time for the source material. But if the *release* time is too quick, the natural decay of the note can get truncated, resulting in a "clipped" sound that most drummers would deem unpleasant. Too long a release, on the other hand, will let in *any* sound that happens to occur during that time, possibly resulting in a leakage problem similar to that described above.

## So Why Gate?

That's a good question, especially in light of what our panel of pros had to say about it. One thing to keep in mind is that, unlike first-call session players, when most of *us* go into a studio we're not going into Little Mountain or Ocean Way (two top studios known for having great drum rooms). Studios like those have meticulously designed rooms boasting absolutely gorgeous ambience. (They usually also have a couple of AKG *C-12* vintage tube mic's—at about twelve grand a pair—to hang over the drums, and probably a pair of Neumann *U-87s* stuck way up in the corners, too!) As recording engineer Ed Thacker says, with such rooms you're actually paying *for* the bleed, so why fight it?

That's understandable, but what about the rest of us? At least early on in our recording careers the odds are that we'll be using more modest facilities. Many of these studios have mediocre (or worse) acoustics, and you might *not* want to include the bleed in your drum sound (let alone pay for it). Eliminating bleed in these instances would be a legitimate use for a noise gate. You might also find a gate handy if you decide to add digital reverb to make up for the lack of room ambience. (More about this in a minute.)

Gates are also used occasionally as an effect, or to process a digital effect ("gated reverb," for example). They can also be used to help lock in other instruments with the drums.

## How And How Not To Gate

Rule number one: Try not to let anyone gate your drums (*especially* your snare) when you're tracking. (The exception is if you're a hired gun, in which case it's the producer's decision. But even then you can suggest waiting till the mix.) Once your drums are gated on tape you're stuck with the results, and if something got left off it's gone for good. Far better to wait until it's time to mix—and even then there are things that can be done to improve the situation.

One method is *frequency-dependent gating*. Most gates have a side-chain input (sometimes called a trigger input) that allows you to use an external signal (other than the source) to trigger the gate. There are several benefits to this, one of which is that you can split a drum signal and

send a "straight" version of it to the gate input and a heavily equalized version of it to the side-chain input. (Don't worry, this won't affect the tone of the gated drum track.) The trick is to set the EQ so it *emphasizes* the instruments you want and *de-emphasizes* those you wish to eliminate. If you boosted the mids and cut the lows and highs on a snare side chain, for example, it would increase the gate's sensitivity to the snare and make it less sensitive to the kick drum and cymbals, yielding much more accurate gating. (Some of the more expensive noise gates have this frequency-dependent feature built into them.)

You can also place an electronic trigger on or in your drum and use this in the side chain. This will help keep other drums from falsely triggering the gate, since the trigger will have more isolation than will the drum mic'. Another benefit of using a trigger with a gate is that it can help you "beat the clock," getting the gate to open sooner than it otherwise would. Here's how: It takes sound waves approximately 75 microseconds to travel one inch through the air. If the trigger is on the drum and the mic' is a few inches above it, by the time the sound reaches the mic' the trigger already has a head start on opening the gate. (And a fast gate will be fully open by the time the mic' signal arrives, so that there's absolutely no truncating of the leading edge of the waveform. This is very important in maintaining the characteristic of the drum's attack.)

You can (and should) EQ the trigger signal to further isolate the sounds you want from those you don't. If you absolutely *must* gate while tracking, this is the setup to use. But even better is to print the trigger signal onto an open track for use during mixdown.

## Applications

Any part of your drumset is a potential candidate for gating. However, unless you're really looking for that over-processed, "early '80s" sound, I certainly wouldn't recommend gating everything on your kit! The main thing is to apply gates only in such a way as to ensure that you're not losing any notes. Part

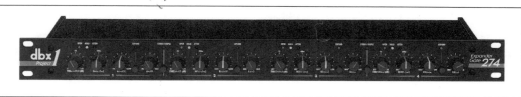

**...the four-channel dbx Project 1 model 274 Expander Gate...**

...and the ART eight-channel programmable Pro Gate.

most snare parts I'd encourage you to use an equalized side-chain signal or a trigger (or both), and to carefully tweak the gate during the mix to ensure that the snare part remains intact. I prefer something even less intrusive, which is to send the dry, un-gated snare off the multitrack straight to the mix, and gate only the reverb send. (Simon Phillips mentioned using a similar technique.) This will still keep your hi-hats out of the reverb, and if a light snare hit doesn't make it through the gate all that will happen is that that particular note won't have any reverb on it—which is far better than losing the note entirely. Additionally, the natural decay of the drum won't get truncated.

of this is using good judgment about which parts to gate (subtle, intricate parts do not lend themselves well to gating) and part is setting up the gate correctly.

We already discussed the importance of proper attack and release times, but the *threshold* setting is equally important. Wind the tape to the softest part of the track (drum-wise) and lower the threshold until the softest hits on the gated drum are just enough to open the gate. If this threshold setting allows undesirable sounds to get through, you have a few options: You can set up a frequency-dependent scheme to increase sensitivity, as discussed. You can keep the threshold where it is and live with the leakage. You can raise the threshold to eliminate the leakage and accept the loss of some of the softer notes. You can elect not to gate that particular drum on that particular track. Or, if the quiet hits are only in one specific section, you can manually "ride" the gate, lowering the threshold during the soft part then bringing it back to where it belongs for the rest of the song.

Some engineers like to gate toms, because they don't like having two or more open mic's around the kit when those mic's may actually be in use for only a small percentage of the total track. Successful tom gating depends on placing the mic's close to the toms and playing fairly solidly. Otherwise the snare will overpower the toms and leak through the gate.

A gate can help create a tight, dry kick sound by eliminating some ring along with the bleed from the rest of the kit. Since kicks are frequently compressed, a gate upstream of the compressor can help keep the noise level down, as well.

When the snare is gated, it's usually because it's going to have reverb added to it, and you may not want that same reverb all over your hi-hats. If the snare part is simply a slamming backbeat on 2 and 4, you're in luck; you can usually just gate it and send it to the reverb and it'll sound fine. But for

If you're recording in a very ambient room you can gate the room mic's (perhaps triggered by the snare and/or tom signals) to create an authentic version of the original "gated reverb" sound popularized by Phil Collins and Hugh Padgham several years ago. And here's a final use for gates I'd like to mention: If the bass guitar track isn't really locked in with the kick drum, you can run the bass through a gate with the kick track plugged into the side chain. This can really tighten things up, since you'll only hear the bass when the kick drum is played (and for a pre-determined time afterward, depending on your chosen release time).

In the final analysis, noise gates are simply tools. As with all tools, they are neither inherently good nor evil—it all depends on how they're used. Gates have gotten a bad reputation due to their abuse by some engineers and producers, and it's true that in the wrong hands they can suck the individuality out of your drum tracks. But used *correctly*, when circumstances call for them, they can help keep things quiet, clean, and tight without destroying the feel of your music.

# Anatomy Of A Gated Drum Note

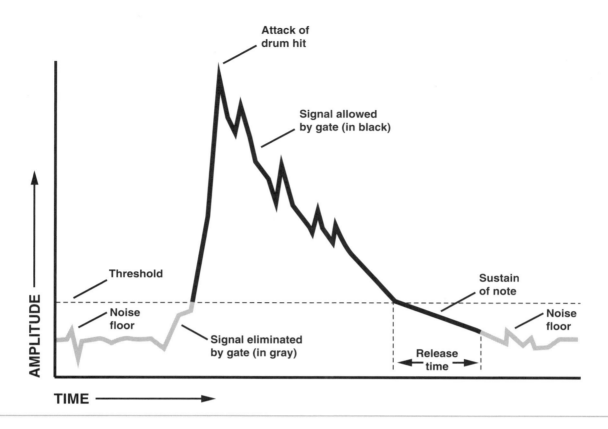

# Fixing A Bass Track With A Gate Sidechain

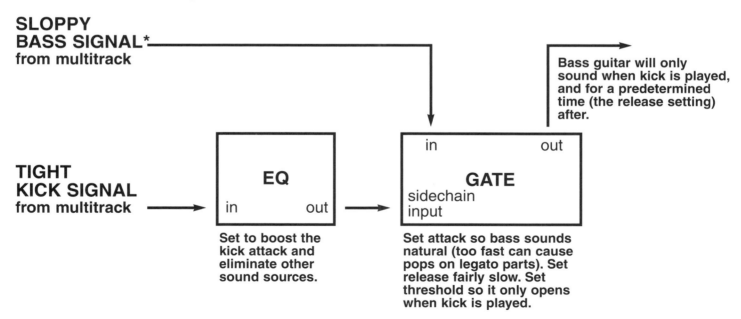

*Note: This technique is primarily used to salvage an otherwise unacceptable bass guitar part (especially when it is impractical to re-record the track) by making it "lock up" with the kick drum. If possible, it is almost always preferable to cut another (tighter) bass track.

# Frequency Dependent/Triggered Gating

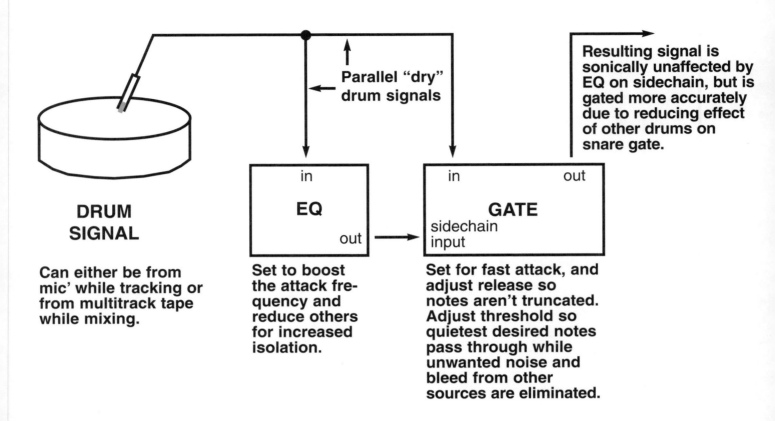

**Parallel "dry" drum signals**

**Resulting signal is sonically unaffected by EQ on sidechain, but is gated more accurately due to reducing effect of other drums on snare gate.**

in EQ out

in GATE out
sidechain input

**DRUM SIGNAL**

Can either be from mic' while tracking or from multitrack tape while mixing.

Set to boost the attack frequency and reduce others for increased isolation.

Set for fast attack, and adjust release so notes aren't truncated. Adjust threshold so quietest desired notes pass through while unwanted noise and bleed from other sources are eliminated.

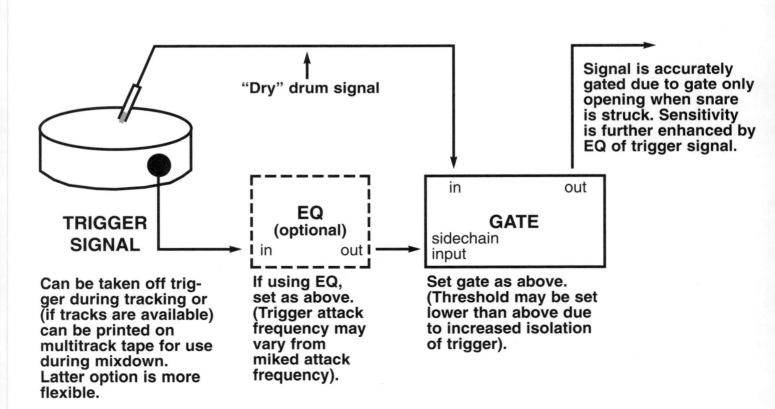

**"Dry" drum signal**

**Signal is accurately gated due to gate only opening when snare is struck. Sensitivity is further enhanced by EQ of trigger signal.**

EQ (optional)
in out

in GATE out
sidechain input

**TRIGGER SIGNAL**

Can be taken off trigger during tracking or (if tracks are available) can be printed on multitrack tape for use during mixdown. Latter option is more flexible.

If using EQ, set as above. (Trigger attack frequency may vary from miked attack frequency).

Set gate as above. (Threshold may be set lower than above due to increased isolation of trigger).

# CHAPTER 9

# Digital Effects

These days there are a whole slew of digital processors available, yielding effects such as reverb, delay, chorus, flange, pitch shift, and harmonize. (Many devices can create several of these effects at the same time.) These are all so-called "time-based" effects, created by digitally sampling the input signal and then sending this sample through an algorithm (a computer program designed to give whatever effect is desired) before spitting the processed signal back out to be mixed with the original unprocessed sound. The unprocessed signal is referred to as the "dry" signal; the processed one is called the "wet" signal.

## Reverb

As drummers we're primarily concerned with ambient effects—those that can put our drums in a pleasing acoustic environment, whether that be a tiled bathroom, a gymnasium, or the Grand Canyon. We're talking *reverb* here.

An almost infinite number of reverb settings are available to you in a modern studio, but don't let that intimidate you. These settings are generally classified by two easily understood parameters: the nature of the room (or space) they're simulating, and their decay time. We'll go into this in more detail, but before we talk about *what type* of reverb to use, we need to decide *which parts* of the drumset we're going to process, and *when* (within the recording chain) we should apply that processing.

## Which Drums?

There are no hard and fast rules about this, but in most types of popular music the snare drum receives the lion's share of the processing. Because it's such a significant part of the mix, the tendency is to make it "bigger than life" by adding digital reverb (or using lots of ambient miking, if you're lucky enough to be recording in a big, gorgeous sounding room). But at the same time there's also a trend—especially in alternative music—back towards a drier sound. Something to remember is that putting a little reverb on your snare has the effect of making your entire kit sound bigger, so that may be all you need to do.

Depending on the music, you may also want to put some reverb on your toms. The huge tom sound frequently heard on power ballads is a combination of a well-tuned drum, a slight boost at the fundamental frequency, and a healthy dose of the

**Single-function processing units include this dbx 290 stereo reverb...**

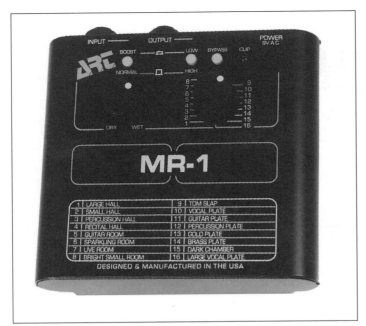

...the ART MR-1 reverb...

appropriate reverb. Also, a little ambience on the toms (of the same type the snare is receiving) will tie the kit together (making it sound as if all your drums were recorded in the same "room"), whereas completely dry toms mixed with a real wet snare may sound "studio-ized." It's a matter of taste.

The overheads don't usually need reverb since they're far enough from the drums to pick up some room sound on their own. (Most folks prefer the pinpoint accuracy of dry cymbals, anyway.) The kick is also usually left dry in order to maximize its punch and precision. However, both of these guidelines can be broken at will. (For example, I've added short, dense reverb to a bass drum on a slow song to increase the boom.) As usual, it pays to experiment.

## When To Process?

At which point within the recording process should we add the reverb (or similar effects)? This partly depends on the nature of the studio you're using. If you're limited to eight or fewer tracks for your total recording, your drums will probably be recorded directly to only two of those tracks. In that case you'll have to add processing as you lay tracks. (This is assuming that you wish to process individual drums. You'll still have the option of processing the drumkit *as a whole* at a later time.)

At larger studios (offering sixteen tracks or more) you should print your tracks dry and wait until the final mixdown to add effects, if at all possible. This not only gives you more flexibility, it also allows you

to see how the drums sit against the finished song, making it much easier to determine the proper type and amount of effects to add.

You may occasionally run into this situation: You have plenty of tracks available, but you're limited to one effects processor—and you've determined that the vocals will need a different type of reverb than the snare. (This is frequently the case.) You can get around this by sending the snare signal to the reverb (prior to mixdown) and returning the reverb output (wet only) to an open tape track. Later, when you mix, you can adjust the amount—if not the type—of snare reverb by adding more or less of the wet-only track to the mix.

## Which Type Of Reverb?

Reverbs are frequently labeled for the type of space they're patterned after. Thus you see programs labeled "small, bright room," "medium chamber," "ballroom," "canyon," and "plate." The last designation emulates a popular type of mechanical reverb created by transducers that were mounted on a large metal plate suspended by springs. Another important spec is the *RT-60*, or decay time. This is the amount of time—measured in seconds—that it takes for the reverb tail to fade into inaudibility (60 dB below the signal level).

Referring to both of these parameters, you'll hear folks refer to a "five-second hall," or a "two-second plate," or a "half-second tile room." Now, Lexicon's two-second plate may be a little different than Yamaha's two-second plate, but they'll be similar enough in general characteristics to serve as a starting place.

*Pre-delay* is another variable that comes into play. This is the short silence (delay) between the input

...and the Eventide H3000-D/SX harmonizer.

Multi-function processors include the Sony HR-MP5...

...the ART FXR two-channel stereo multiple effects processor...

everything else on the multi-track), send some snare signal to the reverb buss, and then scroll through all the applicable reverb programs until I find a few that catch my ear. Then I go back and audition the contenders more thoroughly (frequently tweaking the EQ on the reverb return) until I find the best candidate. Then I bring up the rest of the band and see how the reverb sits with the whole mix. If it sounds complementary, I then set the *amount* of reverb I'll be using. (It's hard to dial in this level until you hear it in context.) Lastly, I'll fine-tune the return EQ, if necessary.

signal (such as a snare hit) and the *onset* of the reverb. It's meant to simulate the audible gap you hear in a large room between the time you hit a drum and the first echo return off the far wall. Short amounts (less than 50 milliseconds) can sometimes be useful in giving your drums a sense of "place," but don't get carried away. Too much pre-delay will have you sounding like you're in a gym. It's really at its best on slow songs where the drumming is rather sparse. On busier tunes it can jumble things up, and the reverb will probably sound tighter and more immediate without it. Here's a hint: If you're going to use pre-delay for that big, cavernous snare sound, set it to a value that relates to the tempo of the song—a 16th note, for example. This'll keep the jumble factor down, and things will sound more musical.

So, which reverb setting should you use? It's ultimately up to you, of course, but smaller rooms and plates with an RT-60 of two seconds or less are popular and sound good on most contemporary music. (Some manufacturers have gone so far as to create reverb programs specifically tailored for drums, with designations like "drum plate.")

What I like to do when looking for a reverb on a particular song is to solo the drum tracks (that is, mute

## Digital Delay

Delay differs from reverb in that it gives one or more distinct echoes instead of a diffuse reverberation. This offers a number of creative possibilities for drummers.

One of the most common applications of delay is to create a "slapback" echo, designed to mimic the sound of early rockabilly recordings. This short echo (approx. 50-100 milliseconds) is usually applied to the snare, but you purists should remember that on a lot of the early mono recordings slapback was used on the whole band!

Using musical values for delay can be interesting. For example, a 16th-note delay on an 8th-note hi-hat part can fill in the holes, creating a 16th-note groove while freeing up your left hand. The same delay set for multiple repeats can really change the feel of a quarter-note kick or snare part. And don't forget about using massive amounts of processing

...the Yamaha SPX990 multi-effects processor...

...and the Alesis MidiVerb 4 18-bit fully integrated extended range signal processor.

on your entire kit as a special effect. (Check out "Bonzo's Montreux" on Zeppelin's *Coda* album.) At the other end, the subtle application of very short delays (say, 10 to 50 milliseconds) can be used to "thicken" tom or snare parts. (Listen to the tom fill on Bowie's "Young Americans.")

## Other Effects

*Chorusing*, along with its cousins, *phase shifting* and *flanging*, was occasionally applied to drum tracks in the past as a special effect, so if you're doing a "retro" project you may want to consider using one of these. (Keep in mind, however, that with most effects of this nature, a little goes a *very* long way.) An updated version of these effects, called *triggered flanging*, is available, where each drum hit re-triggers the flanger to start at the top of its sweep. This can give an aggressive, "biting" quality to snare or tom fills.

*Pitch shift* is another effect found in a number of digital processors. This can make a drum seem bigger (or smaller) than it really is. But again, you have to be careful; if you shift *too* far from the original note it can sound artificial. One way around this is to blend some pitch-shifted sound *with* the original drum sound for more natural results. An even subtler way to enhance your drums with shifting is to apply *pitch shifted reverb*. To get this effect you send a (usually

downward) shifted version of your drum to a reverb, and then return this wet-only reverb to the mix. The result is the original (dry) sound of your drum followed by a big, deep, reverb tail—giving your drum lots of depth without losing any of its initial attack.

## Processing The Processor

You can do wonders for a run-of-the-mill reverb sound simply by equalizing the reverb return a little. In reality, echoes are never as bright as the original sound, so rolling off a little top can make a delay or reverb more natural. In contrast, you can put some shimmer on a sound and keep it from cluttering up

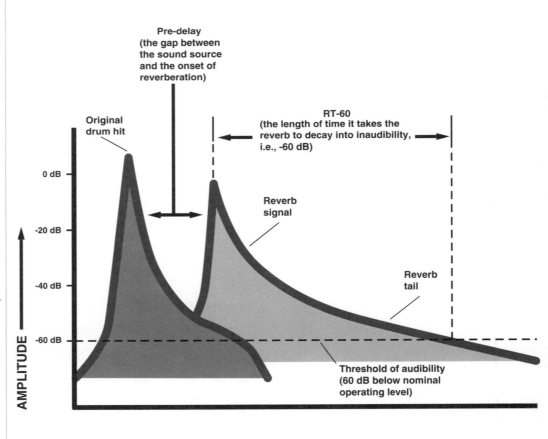

# Reverb Waveform Analysis

the mix by cutting some lows and *boosting* the highs on the reverb. And I'll occasionally put more "bark" into a snare by boosting the *midrange* a little on the reverb return. In each of these examples we've changed the ambient personality of the drum without altering the original sound of the drum itself.

With today's digital processors you can get just about any effect imaginable. But that *doesn't* mean you need to use them all. Think of effects as spices: They can add some zest to the musical meal. But the "meat and potatoes" of a happening drum track is still a good-sounding set of drums, played in a musical fashion.

## Signal Processing

**Q. When it comes to signal processing, are there certain things you like to hear on your drums, or things you like to avoid?**

**Kenny Aronoff:** I'll do sessions where the engineer uses minimal EQ, minimal effects, no gates, and no compression—and it sounds phenomenal. It's all about mic' placement. I like that approach if they can make it sound good. But there are other engineers who add a bunch of stuff to it and it sounds great, too.

The engineer is as important to the whole process as the drummer is. A drummer gets his sound from the way he tunes, the way he hits, what equipment he uses—his whole approach. It's the same thing for an engineer. You can give another drummer and engineer the same gear and it would sound completely different.

**Gregg Bissonette:** One thing that bugs me, EQ-wise, is if the bass drum doesn't have a nice high-end slap on it. Some guys like the bass drum to be sort of flat, but I really enjoy hearing a little bit of that "click" sound on the bass drum. So I often end up asking the engineer, "Is there any way we could put a little more of the click sound in there?"—not overdone, just enough so you can tell what the bass drum's doing.

If I'm going to use reverb, I like to have a large hall reverb—a nice, ambient room sound. The AMS is great for that, and so is the Publison and the Lexicon *224*.

**Simon Phillips:** With some engineers, I just hit the drums, they just put the faders up, and we've got a sound. Others are just not used to that type of process. Usually what happens is they've only got maybe five faders up and they aren't happy with the way the sound is developing. So I say to them "Well look, it's like a grand piano. You have to have everything open before it sounds like anything. You can't just have the first two mic's open and the rest closed." Once they get that concept they put everything up—and then they go, "Ahhh, I see. So *that's* what a drumkit sounds like."

Problems are very rare. Most engineers have good ears and they know what they're doing. It's very occasionally that we come unstuck—and there are two reasons for that. One: very bad acoustics. If the thing sounds bad in the room to start with, there's really not a lot you can do. Two: a cheap mixing board that doesn't have good headroom and doesn't have any NEVE or API channels to put high-transient things like a snare drum and a bass drum through. If you can't get good, expensive electronics that have a lot of headroom before they distort, then you're going to end up with a cheap sound. It just basically compresses and distorts. You don't really hear the distortion, you just don't hear good sound. Tom-toms and overheads are pretty forgiving, but kick and snare have lots of transients, and if you put them through a cheap board it's not going to sound good.

**J.R. Robinson:** I was doing a date with an English engineer. I usually *love* English engineers, but this guy should've been locked up. He was spending so much time on the tom-toms that I thought, "This son of a bitch is gating." I could also hear it being gated in the phones. I said, "Excuse me, why are you gating?" and he said, [affects British accent] "Oh, it'll be a *great* sound. *Trust* me!" I said, "I hate gates. Why don't you get the overall sound of the drumset together, add your overheads, and we will then use less room, no room, some sort of reverb, or no reverb. Why do you need to gate?" The reason guys like him gate is because they can't get a decent bass drum sound or snare drum sound on their own naturally.

As for reverbs, I don't really like gated reverbs. I like short, bright plates with no pre-delay. If I hear pre-delay it throws off my internal clock slightly.

**Q. When you're engineering a session, what are your preferences for signal processing when recording drums?**

**Mike Fraser:** In terms of EQ, I like to record the drums as dry as I can, so that later I can go in and tweak them to get what I want. If you go for a real high-end snare and print that to tape—and then later discover that you need a little more body to the sound, you're stuck.

For reverb, I like to use a lot of the room itself. But if I do need a little bit of reverb effect, I'll use a Lexicon *480* or something similar—short rooms, or maybe bigger halls.

I don't compress when I track. I like to compress the kick and the snare when I mix. Sometimes I also compress the toms, but it depends.

**Ed Thacker:** I might try to EQ the snare a bit to really bring out the tone of the drum. I might also compress various elements of the kit, depending on what we're doing. Other than the room mic's, I don't like to compress during the recording phase because you just never know how hard a guy's going to hit. He might really kill it on one take, and on the next one *not* kill it. You can't change the threshold on your compressor quick enough—so you can get stuck. I might compress the snare and the bass drum a bit in the mixing phase, because a lot of times the right foot can be inconsistent. If you compress it you can get a little more snap out of it and even out the playing a little bit.

**Q. What about gates? How can you keep the bleed down and still not lose ghost strokes?**

**Mike Fraser:** You might want to clean up the snare a little bit—like to try to get the hi-hat out of it. But I try to do that without gating. I hate gating drums. I *like* all the natural rings and rattles.

**Ed Thacker:** You know the way I feel? You're *paying* for the bleed. To me the bleed is what makes recording live drums magical. If you mike the drums properly and the drummer plays with proper dynamics, there's really no need for gating. You can bring out the drum machine if you want all the drums to sound gated.

# CHAPTER 10

# Communicating In The Studio

All right: You've got your drums in shape, you know how to choose a good room (or how to deal with a bad one), you've learned about mic's and their placement, and you've got a handle on equalization and other signal processing. Before you start cutting tracks there's still one more thing you need to think about.

Like any other creative activity involving more than one person, success in the studio depends on *proper communication*. Stripped to the essentials, this consists of two elements. The first is making sure that the picture in your head is the same as the picture in the other participants' heads. The second is making sure that what you have to say doesn't get lost in how you say it. Think of these concepts as *message* and *delivery*, and be aware that they're both vital to getting ideas across. One without the other is worthless.

### Who's In Charge?

The answer to this question will go a long way toward determining how you communicate and who you communicate with. If your band is fortunate enough to get a big-budget deal with a major label, the record company will almost certainly insist that there be an experienced producer at the helm (to see to it that the label gets an acceptable-quality master tape—on time and within budget). If you get called to play on someone else's project there may also be a producer involved. (And even if there isn't

you'll still be working under the direction of whoever's paying you—most likely the artist.) In all of these cases someone else has the final say, and your communication skills will be used primarily in determining what they want and making sure they're satisfied with the result.

However, in most band demos, songwriter demos, self-produced records, and independent label releases (which means the majority of *all* recordings) there is no "official" producer. While the engineer will be the one recording the music, you will be (or *should* be) the one responsible for making the creative decisions about your music—what parts you play, how you play them, and the overall feel and sound of your drum tracks. Congratulations! You've just become a producer, and a large part of your job involves communication.

### Getting Sounds

The job begins the moment you walk into the studio and start setting up your kit. Even if it's your project and you're footing some or all of the bill, you can't introduce yourself to the engineer by saying, "I'm the drummer and I'm here to ensure that you make my drums sound great!" Both the message and the delivery are way off the mark. First of all, arrogance will get you absolutely nowhere. The engineer, whether a highly paid pro or a project-studio amateur, undoubtedly takes as much pride in his (or her) work as you do in yours, and you're killing your chances of a good working relationship by coming off as demeaning and insulting. Also consider that the engineer's idea of a "great drum sound" may be vastly different from yours, so you'll have to do better than that at describing precisely what you're going for.

Descriptive phrases can help, but remember that one person's "bright" can be another person's "harsh." Recorded examples of drum sounds you like can also be helpful tools in getting ideas across. But keep in mind that the drumset on your favorite CD isn't your set, it wasn't played by you, and it was recorded in a different room with different equipment. Probably your best bet is to get the best acoustic sound possible from your kit, and then explain that you'd like the sound on tape to match that sound as closely as possible. As we've mentioned earlier, there will be some discrepancies. (Microphones don't work the same way as our ears do, and they'll be placed in locations you'd never choose to listen to a drumset from.) But this will at least get you and the engineer on the same page. We'll cover ways to suggest improvements in a minute.

When initially "getting sounds" on your drumset, some engineers will focus on individual pieces of your kit rather than on the drumset *as a whole*. Gregg Bissonette brings an attitude to the studio that helps him establish a rapport with the engineer—while reinforcing the fact that the drumset is an integral instrument. Pay particular attention to his comments in the "Ask The Pros" section of this chapter.

## Communication Hardware

**Hearing**. When you start tracking you'll hear the other musicians (and yourself) via a monitor mix fed to a pair of headphones. It's important to the overall feel of the music that you have a good monitor mix, so ask for what you need in the phones. However, be reasonable. While most large studios have a different headphone mix available for each musician, in some smaller studios everyone has to live with the same mix. When this is the case, try to avoid what engineers call the "more me" syndrome, in which each musician demands to hear more of him/herself in the mix. (The same thing can happen—with disastrous results—during the final mix of your recording. We'll discuss this in Chapter 12.)

A workable compromise between the luxury of everyone having their own personal headphone mix

and the "one size fits all" approach is a fairly simple setup that addresses the desire for everyone to hear more of themselves in the mix. This consists of a small box (usually clipped to a mic' stand near each performer) with a few different inputs and a headphone output. Basically, everyone gets the same overall band mix on the first input. Their own instrument is brought up on their second input (with a level control), so they can add as much or as little of themselves to the basic monitor mix as they want. These devices are referred to as "more me" mixers, and they seem to work quite well.

You're not necessarily looking for a balanced, musical mix in your phones. Instead, you're looking for whatever it takes to help you through the song during the tracking process. I don't generally need a lot of drums in my phones. There's always some leakage (even with closed-ear designs)—and besides, I know what *I'm* playing. I'm more concerned with hearing what the *other* folks are doing, so I like to have bass, rhythm guitar, and a guide vocal (along with some kick and sometimes a little snare). If I'm sharing a mix, I usually let the other players decide what they want. Then, if I need more drums, I'll simply pull one of the cups off my ear a little.

Assuming that you do have your own mix, there's no law that says the whole band has to be in your headphones. If it's particularly important that you lock in with a certain instrument, boost it to the exclusion of the others. By the same token, if something's throwing your timing off, pull it down in the mix.

In addition to "more me" cue mixers, there have been some recent developments in headphones that make life a little easier for drummers (and for those who play in their vicinity). I'm referring to "isolation" phones, which feature headphone transducers mounted in shooter's earmuffs. These phones were originally developed to let drummers practice along with a tape or click at lower volume by greatly reducing the amount of outside noise allowed into the phones. But they're also a real boon when recording because they keep the drum bleed out of the mix—making it much easier for everyone to hear what's going on. (And they'll protect your hearing, too!)

**Seeing**. Almost as important as good hearing is good *seeing*. If possible, try to have an unimpeded line of sight between yourself and the other players. If you're using a studio with a drum booth, try putting the guitar amp in the booth instead, then setting the drums up in the main room with the other players standing around you. If done properly, this will give you just as much isolation—and much better eye contact. In lieu of this setup, I've used video monitors a couple of times. They're better than no visual communication at all, but nothing beats everyone playing in the same room when you're trying to capture that "band vibe."

**Talking**. During the session, the engineer and other folks in the control room will communicate with you over the *talkback mic'*, a small microphone on the console that can be assigned to various busses (such as the headphone send or to the multi-track tape). When the talkback is switched on, the control room speakers are automatically muted (to prevent feedback), so you have to wait until they're done talking before you can reply. (If I'm engineering and I'm happy with the sound coming over the speakers, I'll usually put on some phones and leave the talkback permanently open. This permits continuous conversation between the control room and the studio—and seems to help with the flow of ideas.)

The talkback is also used to "slate" songs. The engineer will assign the mic' to the tape and say something like, "'Blues in E,' take 2" so the proper take can quickly be identified on playback. At this point you count off the song. I like to click quarter notes on my sticks for a bar or two before I count, in order to make sure everyone has a solid feel for the tempo. Then, assuming the tune starts on 1, I'll leave off saying the "four" so that there's a nice, quiet pause prior to the music starting. (This makes it easier to edit later.)

*Always* count, even if the song is started by a single instrument. You may want to re-do the intro later or add another part. Having a clear count will make life a lot easier if such a need arises.

## Noise Courtesy

On a related note, due to the technical constraints of communicating in the studio, a certain amount of etiquette needs to be observed. Once the phones are on and the monitor mix is up, any sound that anyone makes is audible to everyone. This means that if the guitarist and the bass player are taking a minute to work out some harmonic details, it's *not* the time to practice double paradiddles. The sort of noodling that musicians sometimes do between songs during rehearsals can turn into a real annoyance in the studio, where it comes over everyone's phones and the control room monitors. On the other hand, if *you* need to work on something pertaining to the recording, just say, "Give me a second to figure something out, please," then do your work. When you're done, say, "Okay, I'm ready. Thanks," and get on with recording. Not to belabor the point, but I've seen things take twice as long (and cost twice as much) just because folks noodled around and didn't focus on what they were doing.

The talkback microphone is the line of communication between the engineer in the control booth and you in the studio.

Using the talkback also requires some etiquette. It's more like conversing over two-way radios than talking on the phone. As stated earlier: When they've got the talkback button down they can't hear you over the speakers, and vice versa. Also, it's important that only one person at a time tries to talk to the engineer (otherwise he won't understand *any* of you). On large sessions it's also helpful if you identify yourself, especially if you're out of the engineer's line of sight. ("This is Fred. Could I have more vocals in my phones?") A lot of this stuff is just common courtesy, but the need is magnified by the logistics of the studio.

### In The Control Room

When you finish the first take, you'll probably go into the control room to hear what it sounds like. What should you be listening for during that initial playback? Not a finished product, for one thing. Your tracks will probably be flat and dry (no reverb or EQ), but that's okay as long as the basic tone is good. With a little experience you'll soon be able to tell if the short, very dry "snap" of your close-miked snare will sound good once it's got some ambience and equalization on it. But if you have any doubts, ask the engineer to add some processing to it during playback (*not* when recording) to give you a preview of how it will sound in the final mix.

The other big thing to listen for, obviously, is the *musicality* of the take. No matter how good things sound production-wise, don't go on to the next step unless everything's also correct musically. Listen with a critical ear for things like tempo fluctuations, timing errors, major dynamic inconsistencies, and that indefinable but all-important *groove*. These are things that absolutely can't be fixed later on.

### Problem Solving

In a certain light, making a recording is nothing more than overcoming a series of challenges: rehearsing the material, getting your equipment in shape, miking your drums correctly, playing with

> **Even if you're footing some or all of the bill, you can't introduce yourself to the engineer by saying, "I'm the drummer and I'm here to ensure that you make my drums sound great!"**

sensitivity and dynamics, capturing the sound correctly on tape, constructing a good-sounding mix, etc. At any stage during the process you can hit a snag, and when you do the success of the project will ride on your ability to get back on track with a minimum amount of damage done in terms of time, money, and attitude.

Speaking of attitude, this has been said before, but it can't be over-emphasized: A positive attitude is key to the success of your recording. This doesn't mean being a "yes man." It means addressing problems quickly in a helpful, non-threatening manner. (Remember that when things aren't going perfectly, the "delivery" aspect of communication becomes more important than ever!) Here are some tips to help you be a problem solver instead of a problem in the studio.

**Concentrate on finding a solution rather than fixing blame**. Upon listening to a playback you notice that the guitar slowed down during part of the song, causing things to sound sloppy. You could look at the guitarist and say, "Hey, man, you were really dragging during the bridge." Or you could try addressing the group as a whole with, "Let's try it again, and this time let's concentrate on keeping the tempo steady through the bridge. I think we might have slowed down a little on the last take."

The first method will alienate the guitar player for the rest of the session, waste time, create a bad vibe amongst everybody, and (if you're insecure) make you feel superior for about thirty seconds. The second method will achieve what's best for the *music*, quickly and without pointing fingers. Does it really matter whose fault it was?

**Make suggestions for improvement rather than negative comments**. If you're unhappy with the sound of your bass drum, you could tell the engineer, "You know, my kick sure sounds like mud," or you could say, "The drums sound pretty good overall, but I'd like to see what the kick would sound like with more beater attack. Can we try that?" I'll leave it to you to decide which would be more productive.

**Be aware of the difference between energy and tension**. *Energy* is a positive feeling resulting from the excitement and challenge of attempting to do something new and creative. *Tension* is a negative emotion coming from anger, guilt, or fear of failure. The differences are pretty clear-cut, but the real key lies in converting tension into creative energy. Let's say your tracking session is almost over, but you'd really like another take of the last song, just in case. This sort of pressure has the potential to create tension, especially if you say something like, "We've only got time for one more take. Let's do it again...and don't anybody blow it!" On the other hand, you could turn the situation around with something like, "We've already got a good take of this in the can, so let's have fun with it this time. Let's just kick it out like we did at the club last week." While the first method *may* get you through the song safely, I'd bet my hi-hats it won't provide any moments of inspired musical creation. The second approach, however, just might get you that killer take you've been looking for. And even if it doesn't, you've still ended on a positive note with everyone looking forward to completing the project.

I'd like to close this chapter with a final thought: Have big ears! *Listen* to the other players—not just when they're playing, but also when they're talking. When someone puts forth an idea—even one you think is unsuitable—listen carefully and consider it seriously. Above all, don't dismiss it before giving it a chance. First of all, when you summarily reject an idea at the outset you're not just quashing one idea, you're quashing that person's willingness to ever offer up another idea again. And second, remember that this is art, not science. There is usually more than one right answer.

## Communication

**Q. What do you discuss with the engineer prior to a session in order to ensure a good drum sound?**

**J.R. Robinson:** As the drummer, I usually have to show up thirty minutes to an hour before the session downbeat. The engineer will usually show up about the same time. If I don't know the artist or what the music is, I'll ask the engineer what we're doing and what kind of music we're cutting.

Fortunately, I've been busy enough over the years that 80% of the time the engineer is someone I've worked with before. He knows me, I know him, and I know how he's going to mike the drums and what selection of mic's he's going to use. I'll immediately offer my suggestions on microphones. If he hasn't used a mic' that I prefer, I'll say, "Would you be willing to try this? It's the greatest mic' you're ever going to use on the bass drum." And he'll say, "Sure, I'll try it."

**Simon Phillips:** It all depends on the guy. We usually say hello, then he sees the drumkit and takes a step back. [laughs] He sees that I've already installed a lot of microphones on it, and what happens is he usually asks *me* questions. If he doesn't know the mic's he'll say, "Hey, what are these? Do they need phantom power or not?" He might ask, "Where on earth am I going to put the snare drum mic'?" We just sort of chat. He'll say, "What do you normally have on the snare drum?" I'll say an *SM57* and he'll say, "Good, it so happens I have one right here in my hand"—that sort of thing.

Although it rarely happens, in some studios I've been to the kit will be miked up with different mic's. For example, they might have Neumann *U87s* on each tom-tom. The engineer usually says, "You know, I saw your mic's but I'd really like to use these." And I'll say, "Great! Six *U87s* on my toms—fine!" But usually we're both experienced enough that not much really gets said—because it's all pretty obvious.

The only other thing I would talk to the engineer about is how to pan the kit, because that is something a little bit different. The first thing I ask the engineer is whether he likes to "look at the kit" or "sit behind the kit." In other words, when you're panning from the console, do you like to have the hi-hat coming out of your right speaker like you're looking at the kit, or do you like to have the hi-hat coming out of your left channel? Nine times out of ten, thankfully, most engineers like to look at the kit. That's the way I like it when I engineer. Although I play the kit, when I'm listening in context, I like to look at a kit. It's very rare I find an engineer who wants to do it the other way around.

Next I tell him I like to pan the kit a certain way because I feel it offers the best spatial area for the kit to sit in. The first four rack toms get panned from hard right to hard left. Let's say hard right is 4:00, then #2 would be 2:00, #3 would be 10:00, and #4 would be 8:00. Tom-tom #5 would be in between tom-toms #1 and #2, and tom-tom #6 would be somewhere around the middle—but not quite central. The gong drum goes in between #3 and 4 so you get a bit of movement. Then the *Octobans* go the opposite way: #1 is left, going to #4 on the right. The overheads are panned hard left to right, with the hi-hats on a separate track, panned in a bit. And that's really all we talk about. After that I just hope he doesn't take too long and doesn't do too much.

**Rod Morgenstein:** Sometimes a particular producer is brought in—either through the suggestion of the record label or because they were hot at the time and you wanted to work with them. In those cases it's almost as if you have to defer to them, because *they* don't really *need* to be there. If you hit them with, "This is the way I do it man, let's get it straight," [laughs] they'll say, "Well then, I guess you really don't need me to be here, 'cause I have *my* own way of doing things."

I've always taken the approach that playing the instrument is my strong point. So although I have my opinions, I assume that a producer or an engineer is a lot more qualified in the area of making things sound good—based on their past performance. But if I were doing my *own* thing, I would try to work with someone who is into taking the time to make the drumset—as it sits there in the middle of the room—sound as natural and as good as it can without enhancing it or replacing it with samples. You can *always* sweeten the acoustic sound of the kit by using whatever effects you have in the studio; there's a never-ending supply of reverbs, noise gates, harmonizers, and things.

**Jim Keltner:** Believe it or not, I usually don't do *any* talking to the engineer, since it's a producer's medium. The producer, along with the artist—depending who the artist is and how much involvement he or she has—generally have an idea of what they want when they call me. So I'll let the engineer do his thing. But I may bring in another piece of gear—something to make the drums sound a little funny or a different instrument to hang on the kit. When I do that I just generally tell the engineer what it's going to be and let him choose and place the microphone. I'm not knowledgeable enough of microphones to tell the engineer to use this or do that.

I've been fortunate over the years to work with great engineers—though I do wish that more engineers would be more adventurous. I do such mainstream stuff that there isn't as much adventure as I would like. People are trying to be competitive and don't necessarily want to try new things. Actually, as I hear myself saying that, I think about all the times I go to a session where people will say, "Listen, what can we do *different* this time?" So there's at least a lot of talk of it. [laughs] Whether it actually happens or not is another story.

The thing I run into all the time is that although I purposefully screw around with my drums just to get a different kind of sound, when I hear the record after the mixing and mastering is done, they've made me sound just like everybody else anyway. [laughs] I don't know what it is—it's a conspiracy in the music world. There are more followers than there are leaders. But it's out of your hands unless it's your project.

**Kenny Aronoff:** My experience with engineers varies. Usually they're very, very cool, and they'll let me set up my drums the way I want—whatever I need to get my sound. What happens is usually I ask *them*: "Do you mind if I keep a front head on the bass drum?" or "Do you want the bass drum to be muffled tight?" Personally I like to use a front head with a small hole and minimal muffling so I get a little bit of ambience. That way the drum doesn't sound like a cardboard box. The other thing I'll ask is: "Do you mind if I use 18" crash cymbals?" Sometimes if they have a lot of room mic's to make the drums sound big, the cymbals will be too aggressive. Other than that they encourage me to do my thing.

**Gregg Bissonette:** The first thing that I like to do is break the ice by saying, politely, "I'm really looking forward to working with you, and I'm sure that we both share the same opinions on a good drum sound." I like to hear as much nice low end on all the drums as possible—but as much high-end slap and crack as possible, too, because I don't like drums that sound muddy and murky. I really like to get a nice, wide open tone, but one that's real fat and really hits you in the chest. When it has that attack *and* it has that fat low end, to me it's really happening.

While I'm setting up and tuning my drums and we're talking, I'll mention the kind of heads I use and the fact that I have RIMS on my drums. I'll talk about my Slingerland kit and how I like to get a nice attack and a nice, warm open tone, and how I don't like to use any tape. I do put a little padding in the bass drum, but basically I like to have the drums really wide open and *ringing*—not *obnoxious* ringing, just nice, fat sustain. And they'll say, "Oh yeah, man, I'm with you!"

One of the other key things is just to make sure that while you're tuning and the engineer is placing the drum mic's, you ask him or her to listen to what your drums sound like in the room. More than anything what I want the engineer to do is make the drums sound true-to-life. A *good* engineer will usually sit and listen. And while the engineer is listening, instead of just playing a bunch of licks or trying to impress somebody, I like to just play real solid time, hitting all the drums and all the cymbals. That way they'll know it's supposed to sound like a *complete* kit.

I'd get real upset if an engineer came right in and said, "I really need to hear a drummer that hits right in the middle of the snare with no rimshots," so I think I'd be offended if *I* was an engineer and a guy said, "Hey look, man, before we even get started, let me set something straight here. I need my drums to sound like *this*...." You've got to work together.

Part of working in the studio is getting along with other people and making people feel comfortable.

**Q. What do you like to hear in your phones when you're tracking?**

**Kenny Aronoff:** It depends on what I'm doing. If I'm tracking with the whole band I absolutely *have* to hear vocals, because I play off of them. I also want the click track if they have it, and then I like to have a good overall mix of everything else. If somebody has bad time then I start mixing that out. If it starts to be a very anal type of situation where I have to play like a drum machine, then that's where I start mixing everyone else out of the headphones. Lots of click and vocals and just enough of the band to hear what's going on. The safest thing with a click track is to play right in the middle; in most cases that's a good starting point.

**Gregg Bissonette:** I like to hear and *feel* the bass drum in my headphones. I don't really need that much snare drum because it's coming through so loud. I like a little bit of the toms and a really good mix of everyone in the room.

My favorite studios are all places where you have your own separate headphone mixer right there. You can dial up your *own* mix, and to me that's the best way to record. It also takes a lot of pressure off the engineer. One of my favorite things that engineers say is, "Okay, I'm going to get up a headphone mix—and you guys can all bitch about it." [laughs] The more you can simulate playing in a room with a band the better off you are.

**Q. What's the best way for drummers coming into the studio to do their own projects to communicate to the engineer about the kind of sound they want?**

**Mike Fraser**: A lot of guys come in and say things like, "I'd like to sound like Bonham." But the best way is to get their drums sounding good in the studio, and then tell the engineer, "*That's* what I'd like my drums to sound like in the control room."

**Ed Thacker:** I suppose one obvious answer is giving examples of records you really love the drum sound on. You're limited, of course, by the kind of drums, the player, and the setting. Those things are impossible to duplicate. But if you can give an example of a record that you really like, that's probably the best thing. A picture is worth a thousand words.

# CHAPTER 11

# Multitrack Recording

Almost all studio recording done these days (and most live recording, too) involves the use of multitrack recorders. Multitracks have anywhere from four to twenty-four tracks (and occasionally more) and come in five different flavors:

*Cassette-based multitracks* have from four to eight tracks, and frequently come as all-in-one mixer/recorder packages. These are excellent tools for bands to use in making demos of their tunes prior to going into a commercial studio. *Modular digital multitracks* (or *MDM*s) such as the Alesis *ADAT* or Tascam *DA-88* are becoming increasingly popular in both project and commercial studios due to their flexibility, relative low cost, and digital quality, as are computer-based *hard disk recorders*. Both of these digital systems are expandable through the linking of multiple units (in blocks of eight tracks for MDMs and four or eight for hard disks). *Open-reel analog recorders* run the

gamut from $\frac{1}{4}$" eight-track machines to "industry standard" 2" twenty-four tracks, while *open-reel digital recorders* (twenty-four tracks or more) are primarily limited to top-flight commercial studios due to their high cost. Both types of open-reel recorders can be slaved together for forty-eight or more tracks.

## Tracks

Everything else being equal, the more tracks available to you the better. This isn't so much an issue of sound quality as it is one of flexibility.

If you're dealing with eight or fewer tracks, you're probably going to end up collapsing your drums down to two tracks—either by recording them to only two tracks initially, or by recording onto half a dozen tracks and then submixing them onto the last two open tracks. Both methods leave something to be

**The Marantz PMD740 is an example of a cassette-based multitrack recorder.**

Modular digital multitrack units (MDMs) include the Alesis ADAT...

Let's briefly look at the most important features.

**Input Channels**. As with the number of available tape tracks, the more inputs the merrier. At a minimum, you'll need as many input channels as tape tracks—plus a few extra. There's usually no problem when recording, because it's rare to record on *all* available tracks at once. The crunch comes during the mix, when *every* tape track requires an input channel. If you're mixing a sixteen-track tape on a sixteen-channel mixer—and you want to use an input channel to process an effects return—you're out of luck. All the inputs are already utilized as tape returns. This is the reason I recommended having a few extra inputs available. (Yes, you could use aux returns or tape monitors, but they're usually not as flexible as input modules.)

**Onboard EQ**. Try to avoid mixing a serious project on a board with only two-band (high/low) EQ. Control of the midrange is just too critical—especially for drum sounds. Three bands of fixed EQ (high/mid/low) is better, but shoot for something with a sweepable (semi-parametric) midrange control if you can. It will really help when you're trying to dial in on a specific frequency to cut or boost. Four bands of onboard EQ—fixed or variable-shelf highs and lows with sweepable low mids and high mids—will put you in fat city.

**Group Outputs**. Also called *busses*, these allow you to send a signal (or a submix of several signals) to a tape track. As an example, your basic stereo mixer has two busses: left and right. Unlike direct

desired when it comes to controlling your drum sound in the final mix.

With the first method you're stuck with what you got when you first recorded your drums. If you later decide that you need more kick drum, you're out of luck. You'll have to go back and start over at the top (including re-recording all the other instruments done up to that point). While the second method affords you some control of levels (and effects) on individual drums when you do the sub-mix, you're still going to be stuck with the inflexibility of having all your drums on two tracks when it comes to the final mix. (And drums usually sound different when you hear them against the finished song as opposed to listening to them by themselves.)

With sixteen or more tracks, however, you can usually put each drum on its own track, allowing you to take advantage of two of the biggest benefits of multitrack recording: *isolation* of instruments, and *overdubbing*. We'll cover both of these shortly, but the primary point is that putting each instrument on its own track is one of the best tools for maintaining control of your sound all the way through the recording process, from the first tracking session to the final mix.

## Mixers

Okay, you're shopping around for a studio to record in, and you have an idea of how many tracks you'll need to capture your sound on tape. Now, what about that other piece of gear that all studios use: the mixing console? What are the requirements here?

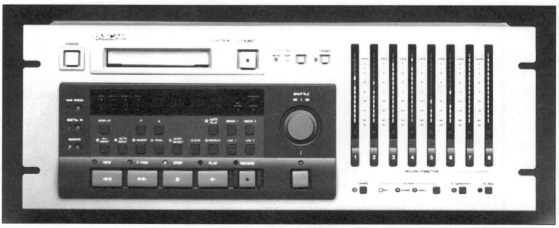

...and the Tascam DA-88.

outs from the mixer's inputs, group outputs limit the number of signals you can send to tape *at any given time*. Currently, mixers with eight or more busses have become the standard for most project and commercial studios. These should provide enough flexibility for most recording projects.

**Aux Sends.** These allow you to route signals to effects processors and headphone cue systems. They are especially valuable during mixdown, when you may be addressing a delay, a chorus, and two or more different reverb programs. I'd consider four to be a practical minimum, with six or more being superior.

The Otari Radar is representative of computer-based hard-disk recorders.

## Pre-Production

One of the best things you can do to help your recording project go smoother and faster (and thus cheaper) has nothing to do with actual recording. It's called pre-production, and by definition it happens before you even set foot in the studio. Basically it consists of having all your musical ducks in a row before you go "on the clock," and it covers a few different areas.

First of all, make sure everything is well-rehearsed. This means more than everybody knowing their parts and being able to play them well (which is, of course, essential). It also means getting all the kinks worked out and giving all the cool little interactions between players that occur over time a chance to develop. (In a perfect world we'd all get to take our songs on the road for six months *before* we tried to record them, but this isn't usually possible. So we do the next best thing, which is extensive "shedding.")

The arrangement details should also be decided on. Experiment with different intros and endings until you find ones that really click. If you're planning on overdubbing secondary parts (like two or more guitar or keyboard parts) you should make sure they're decided on now—and that they indeed work against the primary parts. Don't wait until you're on the clock to audition counterpoint parts. The best way to iron these things out is to make pre-production demos of everything. These can be basic four-track tapes done on a cassette multitrack. Their only purpose is to give you an idea of whether or not the arrangement works.

Another thing that's helpful before going into the studio is to decide on sounds. Many musicians are very picky about their tone, and with all of the options built into modern gear it can take quite a while for them to dial in "their" sound. Obviously, you don't want to pay from $30 to $300 an hour for the privilege of watching someone audition hundreds of synth patches or endlessly tweak a guitar amp. Things will occasionally need to be fine-tuned during the recording process, of course—but the basics should be decided on beforehand. (And by now I don't even need to mention having your drums tuned, right?)

It's also a good idea to make up a dummy track sheet (like the one on page 80) for each song during your pre-production. This is simply a piece of paper divided into squares, with each square representing a tape track. Number the squares, then in each one write exactly what you plan to put on that particular track,

Open-reel analog recorders include the Otari MTR90III.

Modern multitrack mixing consoles include the Mackie 32•8 8•Bus...

(I don't know how many times I've read an interview where someone said they didn't intend to record a given track, but they had some time left at the end of a session so they had recorded it on a whim. And of course that track became the hit.)

You never know, so come prepared. One of your "subs" just might win the game for you.

## Recording Strategy

Planning *how* you're going to record the various parts of a completed song can be very beneficial—in terms of both time saved in the studio and getting the best possible tape of your music. There are endless possible permutations, but we'll discuss the three main methods of tracking here. Then you can fine-tune each to fit your personal needs.

**All at once**. This "live in the studio" method can work great, assuming certain conditions are met. First of all, you must obviously have enough personnel to pull off the entire arrangement. (That is, if you're envisioning three guitar parts, you're going to need three guitar players.) Your band must be *very* well-rehearsed, since any mistakes (or poor performances) by any member will require re-recording the entire piece. Additionally, the studio must provide for adequate isolation of individual instruments from each other—which can prove difficult with things like vocals, acoustic guitars, and pianos.

Provided the above criteria can be met, the "all at once" method can yield recordings that have the ensemble feel of a "live" tape, yet with the superior sonic quality of a "studio" recording. Indeed, some great records have been made this way.

whether it's a cowbell part or an entire horn section. This'll keep folks from getting carried away with the magic of overdubbing and running out of tracks. (I once had a situation where with only two remaining tracks available—carefully left open for a backing vocal and a guitar melody—the guitarist suddenly decided that he wanted to record his part...in three-part harmony!)

Don't forget to give some attention to song selection, either. Naturally, exactly *which* songs to record is an artistic decision that only you and your band (and your producer, if you have one) can make. Just keep the intended purpose of your recording in mind. For example, you might choose different material if you intend to use the tape to shop some songs to a publisher than you would for a release that's already under contract.

The point I really want to make about song selection, however, is to have some backups. Consider your songs like players on a team, with you as the coach. If you were going to take a school basketball team to an away game, you wouldn't only bring your five best players. What if one of them didn't perform up to par for one reason or another? It's the same deal with your songs. If you're making a three-song demo, have at least four songs ready to go. If you need to track a dozen songs for a CD, it would be smart to have fifteen songs worked up. Sure, open with your "starters," but if something doesn't pan out, you'll be able to pull a backup "off the bench." And if things *do* go smoothly, you might have time to record the reserve tunes and pick the best tracks after everything's mixed.

...the Tascam M-2600 MkII...

**One at a time**. This is the opposite of the "live in the studio" approach. Of course, the "one man band" folks *have* to track one instrument at a time, but this method also works well for a band when you're not yet sure of all the details of the song. You can lay down the groove to begin with. Then, after the chord changes have been decided upon, the bass part can be added. The guitarist can then take home a cassette of the bass/drum tracks to help him finalize *his* part, after which the vocalist can do the same, and so on.

...and the computer-operated, automated Otari Status.

(such as a second guitar part or a keyboard overdub), followed by a vocal session where the final lead and backing vocals are cut. Any solos might be tracked next, with things like percussion overdubs and "sweetening" added at the end. The exact order isn't as important as the general concept: Get the core of the band on tape playing as a group, then overdub other parts in a logical sequence that builds on the cohesiveness of the basic tracks. This gives us the advantages of both previous methods: rhythm tracks that have a solid, organic groove (due to interaction between drummer, bassist, and other rhythm players), *and* flexibility for vocals and solos (which can be rehearsed and tweaked against the basic tracks until they feel right). Other benefits include isolation for all overdubbed tracks as well as the use of choice mic's for those same tracks. All in all, this is a practical and highly recommended way for most bands to record.

The "one track at a time" method is also useful if you have to record in a room too small to fit the whole band in at once, or in a room with no provisions for isolation between instruments. The benefits of recording this way are that you can achieve perfect isolation between tracks, and the studio's very best microphones and dynamic processors (which are probably in limited supply) can be utilized on each instrument. The drawback to overdubbing each instrument is that the "feel" tends to suffer. Recordings made this way can sometimes sound more stilted and less organic (especially with regards to rhythm parts) than they otherwise might, due to the lack of interaction during the actual recording.

**Section by section**. This hybrid method uses the best of the two previous techniques. Usually the rhythm section goes first, recording their basic tracks as a unit. To increase the "band feeling" and tightness of the rhythm tracks, the singer usually performs the lead vocal part at this time as well. (This "guide" vocal isn't intended to be part of the final mix. A "keeper" vocal will be tracked later. But the guide—or "scratch"—track helps the groove and makes things easier during any subsequent instrumental overdubs.)

Next might come any additional rhythm parts

Once you're set up to record a basic track, go ahead and cut rhythm tracks for several songs (assuming it's a multi-song project). Then overdub all the vocals, then all the solos, etc., instead of completely finishing one tune before starting the next. This'll save you lots of time and money in the studio. Again, make sure most arrangement details and other creative decisions are made *prior* to entering the studio. (That's why it's called *pre*-production.) Not only is it expensive to rethink your arrangements in the studio, it's also hard to be relaxed enough to be creative when everyone's watching the clock tick away your (presumably limited) recording budget.

Having your arrangements down ahead of time doesn't mean you shouldn't be flexible enough to get alternate takes of a rhythm track once you've got a keeper on tape. This can actually save you time in the long run. For example, suppose you cut a great rhythm track—but your singer thinks the song should be at a faster tempo. Instead of standing around arguing about it, just do an additional take at the quicker tempo. It won't take long (since you're set up for it), and you'll be able to make an informed decision later, when both versions have the vocals and other parts on them. It's always good to have the option, and it's much easier than going back to the studio at a later date to re-record an entire song from scratch.

## The Dreaded Click

Sooner or later you're going to find yourself in a situation where you have to play along with a sequenced instrument, or come in after the fact and lay drums on top of previously recorded tracks. (Or maybe you're just working with a producer who's a fanatic about strict timekeeping.) In any case, you're going to be playing with a click track. It's really not

that big a deal once you get used to it, but *don't* wait until you're under the gun. Start now! Use a drum machine (or just an inexpensive metronome with a headphone jack) and get accustomed to playing with it. For more insight into the subject check out the comments from Rod Morgenstein at the end of this chapter. Rod has created some brilliant drum tracks while working with a click.

Once you're in the studio, if you make sure the click is set up right *for you* you'll have the battle half won. Pick a sound you like—whether it be a cross-stick, a cowbell, a hi-hat, or an electronic beep—and tweak its level until you're comfortable playing with it. You need to be able to hear it clearly, but it shouldn't be distracting. Ideally you should be able to close your eyes and imagine you're jamming with a percussionist who happens to have perfect time.

# Dummy Track Sheet

| 1 | 2 | 3 | 4 | 5 | 6 |
|---|---|---|---|---|---|
| **KICK** | **SNARE** | **HI-HATS** | **TOM 1** | **TOM 2** | **TOM 3** |
| 7 | 8 | 9 | 10 | 11 | 12 |
| (L) | (R) | (L) | (R) | (L) | (R) |
| **DRUM OVERHEADS** | | **ROOM MICROPHONES** | | **STEREO PERCUSSION** | |
| 13 | 14 | 15 | 16 | 17 | 18 |
| **BASS AMP** | **BASS D.I. (Direct Input)** | **RHYTHM GUITAR** | **ACOUSTIC GUITAR** | **GUITAR SOLO** | **LEAD VOCAL** |
| 19 | 20 | 21 | 22 | 23 | 24 |
| (L) | (R) | (L) | (R) | | |
| **BACKING VOCALS** | | **STEREO KEYBOARDS** | | **(OPEN)** | **(OPEN)** |

## Playing For The Tape

Okay, you've found a studio you like, your band's well-rehearsed, you've decided how you're going to track things, your drums are meticulously tuned, and all the mic's have been carefully placed. The red light comes on and you think, "This is it! This is going down for posterity. Everyone's gonna hear it, so I'd better show my stuff...." So you pull out all the stops—playing every fill you've ever learned within the first eight bars of the song in a dazzling display of technique. Right? *Wrong*. More recordings have been torpedoed by over-playing (and under-listening) than perhaps any other factor. A lot of this happens due to the attitude illustrated above, along with a failure to keep the final goal in mind. So here are some thoughts to help you "play for the tape" and achieve a successful recording.

**Songs are built from the bottom up**. I know you've heard this before, but it's true: You can't build a good structure on a weak foundation. The basic tracks—especially the drums and bass—should really feel good before any other parts are added to the song. If you finish a take and *you* know that something about your part wasn't up to par, fess up right then and there. It's far better to invest a few minutes to take another swing at it now than to have everyone realize during the final mix that the groove just isn't happening.

**Always keep the finished song in mind when cutting drum tracks**. When it's just you and a bassist (and maybe a rhythm guitar), there's a lot of space in the music. It's easy to get carried away and fill in all the holes. (This is another reason why it's a good idea to have someone singing a guide vocal when cutting basic tracks.) Whether or not there's a vocal cue available, however, you should envision the completed song and be aware of how your drums fit in. Then be sure you *play* the part you envisioned—even if you end up tracking all by yourself.

**Support the song rather than your ego**. Musicians often come up with parts that they think are interesting or unique—or that simply show them in a good light. They become so enamored of these parts that they're blind to the possibility that they might not fit a song at all. Avoid this syndrome by stepping back and listening to the song as though hearing it on the radio being performed by another band. Does the drum part groove, or is it distracting? Does it enhance the song, or weaken it by competing with a vocal or featured instrument?

If you can't be objective enough to do this while you're actually playing, then listen to rehearsal tapes. As mentioned earlier, it's best to sort these things out well in advance.

**Listen closely to your favorite pro drummers**. You know what they can do when they're burning, but I want you to analyze what they're playing in the middle of a verse or during someone *else's* solo. I think you'll find that even the more technical drummers know when to shine and when to lay down a foundation that makes the music *feel good*.

I don't want to leave you with the impression that "playing for the tape" equals "no chops allowed," because it doesn't. I like listening to a skilled player show his stuff as much as the next drummer. It's just that our goal here is to see to it that when you go into a studio—whether a four-track demo room or a forty-eight-track pro facility—you come out with a tape that both drummers *and* non-drummers like. We also want that tape to be successful at whatever its intended purpose is—from landing you a gig at that club downtown to landing you a deal at a major label.

# Tracking Live In The Studio

This floor plan shows a band tracking live in the studio. By utilizing the isolation rooms for amplifiers (instead of for individual players), the musicians are able to play in close proximity to the drummer in the live room, thus preserving the "band vibe." The singer remains in a vocal booth (due to acoustic necessity). He or she either performs a keeper take (if going for a completely live take) or a guide track (if the purpose of the session is to record a rhythm track). All musicians are monitoring themselves and the others via a cue mix on headphones.

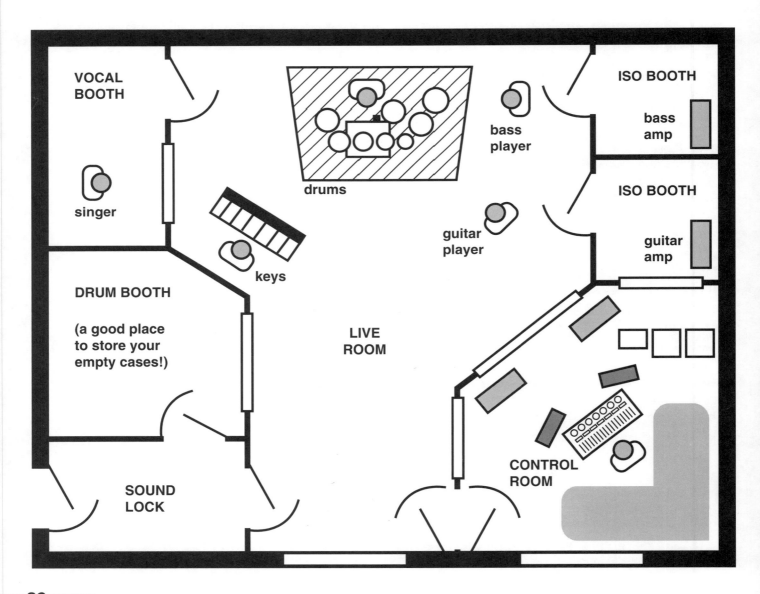

VOCAL BOOTH

singer

DRUM BOOTH

(a good place to store your empty cases!)

SOUND LOCK

drums

keys

LIVE ROOM

bass player

guitar player

CONTROL ROOM

ISO BOOTH

bass amp

ISO BOOTH

guitar amp

## Studio Tips

**Q. Rod, you have a lot of experience at working with a click. Any tips?**

**Rod Morgenstein:** The click is your friend; it's not supposed to be an enemy that embarrasses you and makes you realize how human you are. And like anything, you have to practice with it. If you have no experience with it you're probably going to be very surprised at how difficult it is to play consistently with it. It's like most skills in life: You have to do them consistently to stay at a particular level or get better at them. I can't emphasize enough to drummers who really are serious about a career in music and who hope to get into recording studios that you have to spend *some* of your practice time working with a click, because the odds are that once you get in the recording studio you're going to have to play with one. It's such a competitive business that if you don't do a good job the first time out you're not going to be called back again.

Playing with the click will build your confidence. I think there's a feeling sometimes that if you practice with a click you're going to then become dependent on it, but I don't feel that at all. When you've been practicing with one and then it's *not* there, you're going to take some of that influence with you—some of the consistency of it. It's going to help you start thinking more in time.

As to the *sound* of the click, it depends on the tempo of the song. If it's a fast song, it's nice to have *gonk-gonk-gonk-gonk*. [sings quarter note cowbell] I like a cowbell because it's a cutting sound. A hi-hat is not really good because you're *playing* the hi-hat, and the sounds might get in each other's way. For slower songs I like to have the cowbell and then maybe a stick on a rim—a different kind of sound: *gonk-click-gonk-click*. The other thing to remember is that the more space you have from pulse to pulse, the harder it is to keep it together. When you just have *gonk...gonk...gonk* you're going to have a much more difficult time than if you have *gonk-click-gonk-click-gonk-click*. Even though this can sound very annoying and it's sometimes hard to think musically, the more you do it the easier it gets.

**Q. If a drummer were going to go into a professional studio for the first time, what's one piece of advice you would give him to help him get good tracks?**

**Ed Thacker:** The drums should be tuned well and the drummer should understand about playing with dynamics. He or she needs to understand about the bleed thing, and this is where "inside" dynamics really help. For example, that hi-hat's going to cut no matter what, but if it's all over the snare it makes it really hard to get a good snare sound.

**Mike Fraser:** The best thing is for them to get *their* sound—don't worry about what the engineer's telling them to do. Get the sound that *you're* comfortable playing with, and then tell the engineer, "This is my sound, now get that in the control room." Too many drummers get all worried about sounding like somebody or other. They go out and buy heads that they've never played on before, and then they go into the studio and try too hard—and then their feel goes to hell.

# CHAPTER 12

# The Mix

The final mixdown of your multitrack recording won't involve any actual drumming on your part, but that doesn't mean you can take the day off. You've struggled this far to keep your drums sounding the way you originally envisioned them, so don't slack off now. The mix can go a long way toward either making or breaking your drum tracks (indeed, the entire *recording*), so extra attention is warranted at this stage. Before we get to the nuts and bolts of mixing your tracks, however, let's look at some of the logistics of the process.

## Where?

Although there's a good chance you'll mix your tape at the same place you recorded it, don't automatically assume that this is the only option. The increasing popularity of modular digital multitracks has made it possible to track in a project studio and mix at a pro facility (where they're likely to have a great board and tons of processing gear). The reverse situation also occurs on occasion, where your chosen studio isn't capable of recording live drums so you go to a big room for drum tracks (or entire rhythm tracks), then you go back to the smaller studio for vocals, overdubs, and mixing. If you do end up mixing where you tracked, you'll have the advantage of already being familiar with the equipment, the control-room acoustics, and the monitors—all of which make it easier to make critical decisions when listening to the mix in progress.

## Who?

Here, too, several options are available to you. There are advantages and disadvantages to having various parties mix your tape, so let's examine each of them briefly.

**Professional analog mastering tape decks (like these from Otari's MX5050 series) can add warmth and musicality to your recordings.**

Although digital mastering (on units like this Panasonic SV3800 DAT recorder) has limitations, the medium is quiet and clean and introduces fewer artifacts into the signal chain.

**The producer**. If your project has a separate producer, he's probably a good choice to oversee the mix (although he'll usually have the engineer actually turn the knobs). By this stage, the producer should be very familiar with your music and the direction you want to go in. (Beware, however, of a producer who seems bent on his own agenda without regard for the band's desires.) As an indicator, if you've been happy with the producer's creative decisions during the tracking sessions, you'll probably be in agreement with most of his mixing decisions, too.

**The outside mixer**. This is a person with both production and engineering skills who specializes in mixing. (Bob Clearmountain comes to mind as an example.) If the scope of your project warrants it, you or your producer may decide it's worth it to hire someone specifically to do the mix. On one hand, he probably won't be as familiar with the music as someone more closely associated with the project. On the other hand, he'll be very experienced at mixing and should be able to get a professional sound together in short order. Big-budget commercial recordings frequently use an outside mixer.

**The engineer**. Many independent recordings are done at small studios utilizing an in-house engineer (who may or may not be the studio owner). In this situation bands will often leave the mixing duties to the engineer. On the plus side, the engineer knows the equipment very well (and by now he should be somewhat familiar with the songs). But he really has no artistic stake in the project, and you're liable to get a mix that features his taste in music more than yours.

**You**. (I'm referring to both you *and* the other members of your band, as in "y'all.") Unless you're recording at home on a multitrack cassette machine (in which case self-mixing is probably a necessity), I really wouldn't recommend a band mixing a recording themselves without some additional assistance. First of all, audio engineering is a skill, just like

playing an instrument. The place to learn is *not* on an important recording in which you've by now invested considerable time and money. Yes, you know what the music should sound like more than anyone else does. But without some engineering expertise, you'll have a very difficult time *getting* that sound.

Second, it's always helpful to have the input of someone outside the band who can render an objective opinion when called upon. Without this, chaos can reign. When bands mix themselves, each member usually (and understandably) wants to hear more of his or her own instrument in the mix than the other members deem necessary. This results in the classic "more me!" situation, with each member raising their respective level in the mix until all the faders are at 10, the meters are well in the red, and smoke is coming out of the board—and the lead singer's ears! Time to consider the next option....

**You and the engineer**. This gets my vote as the best method for mixing most projects—especially self-produced or indie-label recordings. Here's one workable scenario: The engineer sets up a basic mix, and the band members indicate what changes they'd like to hear—which the engineer then carries out. The musicians then re-evaluate, the engineer tweaks some more, etc. This method can quickly result in a professional-sounding mix (due to the engineer's involvement) that still reflects the unique vision of the band (due to your detailed input). Also, the engineer can act as an informed referee should a difference of opinion arise.

## Which Format?

Deciding which format to mix to is an artistic as well as a technical decision. Analog and digital each have their own particular qualities, which actually complement each other quite well. For this reason you should consider mixing to analog if you tracked on digital, and vice versa.

There are several new products on the market that are designed specifically to add analog-type qualities to digital recordings—for good reason. Pro analog mastering decks ($1/4$" or $1/2$" open-reel half-track machines running at 15 ips or higher) can add a certain warmth and musicality to your recordings that's hard to get elsewhere. Printing "hot" levels on analog tape results in "tape saturation," which slightly compresses and fattens the signal in a way many people find pleasing (although too much of this leads to audible distortion). It's also easy to sequence your songs (place them in correct order, with desired spacing between songs) on an analog machine without the need for a second deck to bounce to. If you need to send out a digital copy for duplication (which is very likely), you can easily make a DAT copy, retaining the benefits of mixing to analog.

Digital, on the other hand, is a very quiet and clean medium that introduces fewer artifacts into the signal chain. If you tracked on an analog multi-track (with presumably healthy levels), you've already received the previously mentioned benefits. In that case, it makes sense to skip an additional analog generation and mix directly to digital. However, since you can't cut and splice DAT tape, you have to come up with other methods of sequencing your songs. Here are three or four options.

You can mix your songs in their final order directly to the DAT master. This is the least-desirable method, since it gives you no flexibility—but it may be necessary due to equipment limitations. If two DAT machines are available, you can mix to one and sequence to the other. (This keeps you in the digital domain while sequencing, which avoids another pass through the analog-to-digital converters—the weak link in most digital systems.) If two DATs aren't available but the studio has an MDM, you can mix to two tracks of the MDM and sequence to the DAT or another MDM. If a hard-disk system is available, you can transfer your stereo master to it and use it for sequencing—a task for which computer-based systems are extremely well suited. If the final goal of your recording is a CD, mix at a sampling rate of 44.1 kHz— even if higher rates (like 48 kHz) are available. CDs are made at 44.1 kHz, and you want to avoid a potentially degrading sample-rate conversion. So start at the rate you're going to end up with and stay in the digital domain thereafter.

If the option of using a synergistic combination of digital and analog isn't available to you, don't despair. Think of all those great-sounding records in your collection that are all-analog. At the same time, remember that a large number of today's best-sounding CDs are digital from start to finish. Gear *is* important, but it's not *as* important as the people using it.

## When?

In reality you start work on the final mix as early as the pre-production phase (when you make up a track sheet for each song), and during each session along the way (when you make a note whenever you get an idea about how you'd like things to end up). For example, if during tracking you visualize huge drums on part of the song, write "big reverb on toms during bridge" on the track sheet *right then*. (Define thy vision…remember?)

As for the actual mix, there are a couple of ways to schedule it. If you're doing very simple arrangements (such as "songwriter demos"), you can mix as you go. This involves recording a song, immediately mixing it, and (assuming you're happy with the results), going on to the next song. For anything more involved, however, your best bet is to do the tracking for all the tunes before starting to mix. There are two reasons for this.

First, once you've got the board and all the outboard gear set up to record, the most efficient thing to do is to record everything, since it takes quite a bit of time to set the correct levels and patch everything together. The same goes for setting up to mix. Second, a similar philosophy applies to your mental attitude. When you're recording you should be primarily concerned with musical matters. (Was that part tight? Were we in tune? Did I rush?) But during the mix you put on your "mix ears" and think about sonic things. (Is the

Large, far-field monitors (like the JBL/UREI 813C models shown here) are important for checking bass frequencies, but they can give an unrealistic impression of the total mix.

vocal loud enough? Does the bass guitar need compression? Is there too much reverb on the snare?) It's difficult to switch back and forth rapidly.

## Ear Calibration

The engineer will calibrate the various machines, but before you mix *you* must calibrate your ears to the mixing environment (that is, everything in the playback chain, including the amps, the room, and especially the speakers). The easiest way to do this is to bring in some CDs you're familiar with (ideally in the same style as the music you'll be mixing) and listen to them in the control room. This will give you a reliable indication of the tonal character of things, and you can adjust your mix accordingly. If your favorite CD sounds a little bright on the monitors, that's okay—you aim for the same high frequency content in your mix, and so on. Refer often to your reference CD throughout the mixing process (for subtle things like relative level of instruments, as well as EQ) and it'll help keep you out of trouble.

## A Word About Speakers

Most studios have at least two pairs of monitors: a large pair (far-fields) usually mounted in or on the front wall of the control room, and a smaller pair (near-fields) above the console. Even though the big guys can put out chest-shaking levels and are a lot more exciting to listen to, you're probably better off doing most of your mixing through the near-fields. This is simply because the big speakers probably sound different than what *you're* used to listening to, and—more importantly—because the small speakers are probably a lot closer to what most people are going to listen to your recording on.

Even experienced engineers will spend most of their time on the near-fields. They'll switch to the large monitors for two purposes: first, to check the bass frequencies (the big speakers go lower, allowing you to tell what's going on in regions that the smaller speakers don't reach), and second, to impress clients. Don't fall into this category by allowing yourself to be taken in by the "bigger than life" sound of large monitors. Sure, it's a thrill to hear your drums coming back at you at 110 dB with your kick sounding like a cannon and your snare like a gunshot. But the point isn't just to make your drums sound great in the control room; it's to mix them so they sound great on whatever system they're played on. For that the near-fields are usually the better bet.

Studio near-fields aren't without their own little quirks, however. They're designed to be listened to very closely (head-high, and maybe three feet from your ears, with the two speakers and your head forming an equilateral triangle). Additionally, some models don't sound much like typical stereo speakers, which is why it's important to get familiar with them prior to mixing. If you find yourself trying to mix on monitors that sound bizarre and unmusical to you no matter *what* you do, consider bringing in a pair of your own speakers with which you're already very familiar. They probably won't be as accurate (technically speaking) as the studio monitors, but at least you'll know what you're getting and you won't feel adrift at sea without an anchor. Another option (actually recommended in any case) is to take rough mixes home after each day's work and play them on your personal sound system—preferably side-by-side with familiar recordings. This is a great way to double-check that you're on the right track.

**Your mix should also be carefully considered through small, near-field speakers, like this Yamaha NS10M...**

**...or these Audix 1A models.**

# The Process

No matter how you like to build your mixes, it's helpful to have a basic game plan to follow for each song. I'll present a general outline that I've found useful, but feel free to modify it to suit your needs. No, you can't learn to be a mixing engineer in the course of one chapter, but there's one thing you're more of an expert on than anyone else in the studio: how *your* drums should sound. Always keep this in mind, and don't be afraid to speak up if you detect something amiss with your sound.

Before you heat up the speakers, here are some tips regarding your ears. Set the monitors at a moderate level, and *keep* them there. If you mix at high volume, your ears will become fatigued in short order—and you'll find yourself adding increasing amounts of high end in an attempt to compensate. (If the mix is so bright the next day that it tears your face off, that's a sure sign your ears were toast when you mixed it!) Take frequent breaks—at least every two hours, if not more often. Even at moderate levels your ears start to attenuate the high frequencies over time. Your brain needs a rest, too. Listening to the same track for several hours without a break can render the song an indecipherable mess.

In the end, what matters is how your kit sounds against the completed song. However, on my way to that goal I try to optimize each part of the drumset before adding it to the mix by listening to it solo and getting it in the ballpark sound-wise. Throughout the book we've discussed all manner of processing: EQ, reverb, delay, noise gates, compression, and limiting. This is where it all comes together. (We're not going to go into great detail about specific processing again, other than to indicate where it might be appropriate. You may want to review those chapters if you feel you need more in-depth info.) That said, let's go through a sample mix.

First, bring up the kick drum, pan it to the center, and listen. It should sound punchy. If it doesn't, try cutting some lower mids as well as boosting the top end to increase the beater attack. The fundamental should be strong, but not so much that it booms. (The bass guitar will help fill in the bottom, so leave some room for it.) If the sound needs to be tightened up or lacks dynamic consistency, add compression.

Next bring up the snare, also centered. To bring out the snare wires, boost the high end a little.

Need more or less stick attack? Adjust the upper mids. Sounding boxy? Pull out some lower mids. To thicken or thin the overall feel of the drum, tweak the fundamental up or down a bit. (Go ahead and experiment with these and other EQ schemes, but try to end up using the smallest amount you think you can live with—it'll hold up better in the long run. If in doubt, go hit your snare drum. *That's* the sound we're aiming for.) Set up a reverb sound for the snare, keeping in mind that the slower the tempo, the more 'verb you can get away with (and vice versa). If the hi-hats have bled excessively onto the snare track, try gating the reverb send from the snare (instead of gating the snare itself). Now that you've got a reverb sound you like, turn it down until the rest of the drum tracks are in the mix.

Bring in the overheads, panned hard left and right. Assuming you've close-miked the toms, and that the overheads are primarily for the cymbals, try rolling off the bottom end and adding a tiny bit at the highest frequencies. Bring in the hi-hats, panned at three o'clock (or nine o'clock), and give them the same EQ as the cymbals. (A word about panning: You can set up the left/right perspective from either the drummer's or the audience's point of view. That is, either the small tom and the hi-hat to the left and the floor tom/ride cymbal to the right, or the other way around. I prefer the drummer's perspective, but it's your call.)

Put up the tom tracks, panned appropriately. To get a nice fat sound, pull out some mids, and if necessary boost the fundamental (for sustain) and the top end (for cut). Bring in the room mic's, if available, panning them hard left and right and adding whatever EQ is necessary for a big, warm sound (usually a reduction in the lower mids).

Now sit back and listen to the whole drumset, paying particular attention to the relative volume of the individual pieces. The snare should be the loudest part of the kit, cutting with snap and authority, with the kick close behind in terms of level. The toms should sound full (as opposed to thin and wimpy), but not as hot as the snare. The cymbals should be relatively low in the mix—they should sparkle rather than splatter—while the hats can be a bit louder than the ride cymbal as long as they don't come across as being harsh. Add just enough of the room to give the kit a feeling of natural ambience—too much and it'll sound washy and indistinct. Now you can determine the general amount of reverb needed (if any) on the snare and/or toms. Proceed with caution—tons of cavernous reverb may sound exciting when you mix, but I can almost guarantee you'll hate it in six months.

At this point listen to the drums as a single instrument. Do they blend well, or does something stick out due to its level, EQ, or other processing anomaly? If so, now's the time to make adjustments. The goal is to have it sound like an integrated set of drums rather than a collection of unrelated instruments.

Add the bass guitar and see how it sits with the kick. They should lock up sonically as well as rhythmically, with the kick providing the initial attack and fundamental and the bass giving the melodic sustain. EQ tweaks may be in order here, as well as some compression to tighten up the bass. From this point on every mix is different, due to varying instrumentation and arrangement. However, in general the rhythm instruments (guitars and/or keyboards) should be next, using panning and different EQ to separate them if there's more than one. Of primary concern here is to avoid an abundance of midrange buildup, since we must leave room for the vocals.

The lead vocal is next, front and center. This is where most of the listener's attention will be (assuming we're mixing a song with vocals, of course), so everything else must be supportive of it. Can you clearly hear the singer during vocal passages? If not, rethink the dynamics and/or EQ of the other parts. If things have been done correctly, the instruments will be strong *and* the vocals will be intelligible because you've left room for everything, both in the frequency spectrum and in the arrangement. Next are any solos (which are given the same prominence in the mix as the vocal), followed by backing vocals and any instrumental sweetening.

## Wrapping It Up

Once you've finished your mix, do you immediately send it out to the record label, the duplication house, or wherever its final destination may be? Not if you can help it. First you should completely get away from it for at least a few days (and longer if you can). You've been so close to it for so long that it's hard to be objective any more, hence the need for a break. Following that break, go back and listen to the mix on as many different systems as you can: your stereo, your friends' stereos, your car stereo, your *Walkman*, etc. (Heck, take it to a high-end stereo shop and listen to it on their best system!) The point is that a good mix will sound good (or at least acceptable) on whatever system it's played on.

Also consider letting other people listen to it, and getting their feedback. I'm not talking about your next-door neighbor who hasn't bought a record in ten years. I'm talking about musically inclined folks—like other musicians, studio personnel, and serious music lovers who listen to current releases and thus have a production benchmark by which to judge. Even with such informed listeners you'll likely get a barrage of differing commentary. Some will absolutely love it, and some won't care for it. Some won't be able to see past the production to the music, while others will be clueless about the production but will pick on the tiniest of musical details. You can safely ignore all of these varied responses. What you care about is when you hear the *same specific comment* from a high percentage of listeners. (In other words, if some folks think it's "too alternative" while others think it's "too commercial," so what? But if *everyone* says the vocals are buried in the mix, you might want to pay attention.)

If, after living with the mix for a while, you determine that there *is* a fairly serious problem, don't feel too bad. Schedule a remix, and consider yourself fortunate that you caught the problem before you sent the mix to Someone Who Matters. If the mix itself is good, but the overall tonal balance is slightly off (too dull or too thin), you can often fix the situation with the application of a little corrective equalization. (I emphasize the word *little*.) Enhancers really earn their keep in these sorts of situations.

All this tweaking and second-guessing is fine, up to a point. Just keep in mind that sooner or later you have to call the damn thing done. And when it's done, it's *done*. Avoid the temptation to go back six months down the road and have another crack at it. You're far better off to put your energy into your *next* recording project—which will go a lot smoother for having done this one. After all, no mix can make bad music good. The goal of a good mix, like the goal of everything we've discussed throughout this book, is to help good music—*your* music—sound as good as it can.

Happy drumming!

# Glossary

**Absorption**—The acoustic quality of soft, thick, porous materials. They absorb the sound and don't reflect it back into the room. (Also see *Diffusion* and *Reflection*.)

**Ambience**—The overall sonic contribution made by the room and everything within it. Can be characterized by quality (bright, warm, dark, etc.), quantity (live or dead), and length of decay (long or short).

**Anechoic Chamber**—A room scientifically designed to have no reflections, generally used for acoustic research and development. An anechoic chamber would be a poor place to record drums.

**Attack**—The sharp, defining part of a waveform that gives it articulation, occurring at the beginning of the note. With drums, the attack is due to the sound of the stick or beater against the plastic head. (See *Sustain*.)

**Attack Time**—The speed with which a dynamic processor (compressor, limiter, or gate) acts on the incoming signal once the signal has exceeded the threshold. On manually controlled processors this is determined by adjusting the attack control. (See *Release Time*.)

**Aux Sends**—Auxiliary busses, usually on input channels of mixers, that allow you to send varying amounts of the signal to effects processors, headphone mixes, etc.

**Bass Roll Off**—A high-pass filter (with either fixed or switchable corner frequencies) found on some microphones, allowing you to reduce ("roll off") the lower frequencies to eliminate handling noise and popping, as well as to change the sonic character of the mic's response.

**Bleed**—Leakage of sound (usually unintended) from one sound source into a microphone placed on another sound source.

**Buss**—A subgroup on a mixer used to send multiple signals to a common destination (such as a tape track).

**Cans**—Slang for headphones.

**Cardioid**—The polar pattern of a unidirectional microphone, having the greatest response in front, diminishing somewhat at the sides, and greatly reduced at the rear. A graphic representation of this pattern looks heart-shaped, hence the name. (Also see *Hypercardioid*, *Omnidirectional*, and *Figure 8*.)

**Chorus**—A digital effect based on a short delay with variable modulation, this can make a single instrument or voice sound (somewhat) like multiple copies of itself.

**Coincident Pair**—A method of stereo miking using two mic's in front of or above the source with their capsules at an angle to each other (between 75° and 135°) and almost touching. Also known as XY miking. (See *Spaced Pair*.)

**Compression**—Reducing the overall dynamic range of a signal by applying a device (a compressor) that lowers the peaks in the signal. Judicious use can enhance ("fatten") a drum sound.

**Compression Ratio**—The ratio by which the level

of a sound exceeding the compressor's threshold will be reduced. (For example: at a 4:1 ratio, a peak 8 dB above the threshold will be compressed to only 2 dB above the threshold.) The ratio is usually adjustable via a control on the compressor's front panel.

**Condenser**—A class of microphones based on capacitance, requiring either internal batteries or power from an external source ("phantom power"). Usually more sensitive than a dynamic mic', with a flatter curve and better transient response.

**Cue Mix**—Any mix that exists for the purpose of guiding the musicians as they perform. Usually sent via headphones.

**Delay**—A repeat (single or multiple) of the original signal after a predetermined amount of time; an echo. Also refers to any processor that creates such an electronic delay.

**Diffusion**—The scattering of sound in various directions by variegated (non-planar) surfaces. (Also see *Absorption* and *Reflection*.)

**Direct Sound**—Only that sound coming directly from the source, without benefit of any reflections from the room. Usually characterized as thin and dry. (See *Reflected Sound*.)

**Dry**—Without any processing—especially without reverb or other ambient effects. (See *Wet*.)

**Dynamic Microphone**—A microphone of moving-coil design. Generally rugged and able to take high sound pressure levels (SPLs), but without the flat response and extended high end of a condenser.

**Echo**—An acoustic delay caused by a discrete reflection or an electronic simulation of same.

**Engineer**—A person with comprehensive working knowledge of recording equipment who can utilize mic's, recorders, mixers, and signal processors to achieve desired technical results. (See *Producer*.)

**Enhancer**—A class of signal processors that add "intelligibility" and perceived clarity to an audio signal by applying phase correction and/or program-dependent EQ. May also contain provisions for fattening bottom end.

**EQ**—Equalization. The amplification or reduction of selected frequencies. Bass and treble controls are a simple form of EQ. (See *Graphic EQ* and *Parametric EQ*.)

**Far-Field Monitors**—Large, accurate studio monitors with an extended response (especially in the bottom end) meant to be listened to from a distance. Useful for checking the lower octaves of a recording and for putting out high sound pressure levels (SPLs) that "excite" the room.

**Figure 8**—Polar pattern of a dual-diaphragm microphone in which the response is strong at the front and rear but greatly diminished at the sides (like placing two directional mic's back to back). The polar response thus created looks like an "8." (Also see *Cardioid*, *Hypercardioid*, and *Omnidirectional*.)

**Flange**—A digital effect recreating the results achieved when two copies of the same recording are played back at the same time, but with a very small time offset. Similar to a chorus effect, but much stronger.

**Flat**—Any piece of equipment with a linear response curve is said to be "flat." Also describes the condition of any signal to which no equalization has been added.

**Flutter Echo**—A phenomenon caused by two parallel hard surfaces facing each other, so that any sound created within that space bounces back and forth several times, resulting in multiple echoes that decay with a fluttery sound.

**Frequency Response**—States the ability of a piece of equipment to accurately reproduce an input signal, as defined by the upper and lower frequencies it can produce within a given linearity of the original. (Acceptable dynamic variance is commonly plus or minus 3 dB, but not always). Usually given as three figures: the lower frequency, the upper frequency, and the linearity within that range. (For example: "40 Hz—18 kHz, +/-3 dB.")

**Gating**—Using a noise gate to eliminate the quieter parts of a signal by "gating out" or shutting off the signal once the level falls below a predetermined threshold. Sometimes used on drum mic's to eliminate bleed from other sound sources. Overuse can hurt drum tracks by unnecessarily eliminating quiet (but musically important) notes.

**Gobo**—Small, portable panels that can be placed between instruments to reduce leakage.

**Graphic EQ**—An equalizer divided into several frequency bands (usually from 10 to 30), with a separate slider controlling the amount of boost or cut for each band. The sliders are arranged next to each other from low to high frequencies, so that a glance at the front panel provides a picture (graph) of the approximate response curve.

**Guide Vocal**—A vocal part that is sung as other instruments are being recorded in order to provide a cue (guide) for the musicians. May be recorded during its original performance for similar use during later overdubs, in which case it becomes a "scratch" vocal. (See *Scratch Track*.)

**Half Track**—A professional-quality, open-reel mixdown deck with the tape divided into only two tracks (as opposed to the four actual tracks of a conventional stereo cassette or open-reel deck). Each track takes up approximately half of the available tape width, and the tape can be played in only one direction.

**Harmonizer**—A digital processor that can produce musically useful harmonies of the input pitch. Basically an "intelligent" pitch shifter.

**Headroom**—The ability of a device to handle signals above its nominal operating level without distortion. Adequate headroom is especially important when dealing with signals having a wide dynamic range, such as drums.

**Hypercardioid**—A unidirectional polar pattern similar to cardioid, but with a tighter pattern for even greater rejection of sounds coming from the sides, though with a small response lobe directly at the rear of the mic'. (Also see *Cardioid*, *Omnidirectional*, and *Figure 8*.)

**Hz**—Short for Hertz, the unit used to measure sound frequency. One Hertz equals one cycle per second. (See *kHz*.)

**ips**—Abbreviation for "inches per second," the unit used to measure tape speed. Stereo cassette decks run at $1\frac{7}{8}$ ips, cassette multitracks run at $1\frac{7}{8}$ and/or $3\frac{3}{4}$ ips, consumer-stereo open-reel machines typically have speeds of $3\frac{3}{4}$ and $7\frac{1}{2}$ ips, while professional recorders run at 15 or 30 ips. Generally speaking, faster is better, though there is some disagreement about this. (Many engineers feel that 15 ips gives a fatter bottom end than 30 ips, though at speeds below 15 ips the high end suffers noticeably.)

**Indie**—Short for independent record label. Applies to all labels that are not a division of one of the major record conglomerates. Indies range from "Mom and Pop" operations to substantial organizations.

**Keeper**—A good take—one that will be used in the final mix.

**kHz**—Short for kiloHertz, with one kHz equal to a thousand Hz. (See *Hz*.)

**MDM**—Abbreviation for "modular digital multitrack," applying to digital recorders such as the Tascam *DA-88*, the Alesis *ADAT*, and all variants of these models as made by other manufacturers.

**Mute**—To remove one or more inputs from a multitrack mix. Also refers to the button on the input module that performs this function.

**Near-Field Monitors**—Small or mid-sized (typically two-way) studio monitors designed to be listened to from a close distance. One of the benefits of near-field listening is that it increases the direct sound of the speaker as compared to the room reflections, thus eliminating many of the acoustic anomalies of the room from the mix. (Thus you can still accurately mix in a less-than-perfect room.)

**Omnidirectional**—The polar pattern of a microphone that picks up equally well in all directions. (Also see *Cardioid*, *Hypercardioid*, and *Figure 8*.)

**Pad**—Switchable attenuation (typically 10 or 20 dB) on a microphone or input section of a mixer. Used to reduce high input levels (such as from close-miked drums) to more manageable levels.

**Pan**—To place a sound in a certain location within the stereo field. Panning something hard left, for example, means placing it so it only originates from the left speaker in a stereo mix.

**Parametric EQ**—An equalizer that offers variable control over all three fundamental parameters: center frequency, bandwidth, and boost/attenuation. A high-end recording console will typically have fixed high and low shelving EQ with two bands of parametric EQ—one for the low mids and one for the high mids. Related is the "sweepable midrange" EQ, in which the central frequency and gain is variable but the bandwidth is preset.

**Phantom Power**—A low-voltage (usually 48 volts), direct-current (DC) power source supplied by a mixer or outboard device to power condenser microphones (and some active direct boxes). The power is supplied via the mic' cable itself, yet is transparent to the audio signal coming from the mic'—hence the name.

**Phase Cancellation**—An acoustic effect (usually undesired) that occurs when two mic's are at different distances from the same source and one is picking up the sound out of phase with regard to the other. The result is a thin, hollow sound. Solutions are to reverse polarity on one of the mic's (placing it 180° out of phase from where it was previously), or to move either of the mic's until the effect disappears.

**Pitch Shift**—A type of signal processing in which the original sound is digitally shifted up or down in pitch, with the resulting signal either used on its own or recombined with the source sound. This process can be used to fatten the sound of individual drums, or for a special effect.

**Plate**—A type of electro-mechanical reverb, using transducers mounted on a large metal plate suspended by springs. Also refers to programs on modern digital reverbs that attempt to replicate the sound of a real plate reverb.

**Pre-Delay**—In digital reverb, a short delay between the sound source and the onset of reverberation. Simulates the short (but audible) pause you hear in a large room between the time you make a sound and the time you hear the sound reflected back to you.

**Producer**—The person with overall responsibility for creative and technical decisions during a recording session (similar to the director on a movie set). May have an engineering background, a musical one, or (ideally) both. (See *Engineer*.)

**Reflected Sound**—That portion of a sound that has reflected off the interior walls and objects within a space before reaching the listener. The "room sound." Can add apparent size and depth to a sound. (See *Direct Sound*.)

**Reflection**—The acoustic quality of hard flat surfaces. They bounce sound back into the room, creating discrete echoes. (Also see *Absorption* and *Diffusion*.)

**Release Time**—The speed with which a dynamic processor will stop acting on a signal (will "let up," in the case of a compressor, or will close the gate on a noise gate) once the level of that signal has dropped back below whatever threshold caused the processor to act originally. On manual devices this is set by adjusting the release control. (See *Attack Time*.)

**Resonant Frequency**—If a room has two or more dimensions that are the same or multiples of each other, a note whose wavelength is equal to the common room dimension will be accentuated, causing the room to resonate. Also known as "room boom."

**Reverb**—Reverberation. A wash of diffuse sound reflections, as opposed to discrete echoes. Also refers to any device—mechanical, analog, or digital—that artificially generates reverberation.

**RT-60**—The specification on a reverb program that indicates how long it takes the reverb tail to decay to inaudibility (60 dB below the original level).

**Scratch Track**—Any recorded track that is not intended for the final mix, but rather to provide cues for those making subsequent overdubs. Also used to check whether or not a particular arrangement "works" before proceeding further.

**Side Chain**—An insert point in the circuitry of a dynamic processor that lets you access the detector circuit with one signal for use in processing another

signal. For example, you can gate a bass guitar track using the signal from a kick track in the side chain, locking the bass in with the kick. Also used for frequency-dependent gating, gating with a trigger on a drum, and "ducking" (triggered compression).

**Slapback Echo**—An acoustic delay caused by a reflection off of a far wall, especially a parallel wall with a hard surface. Also refers to a similar type of echo created by electronic means. Used on different types of music, slapback is extremely popular on rockabilly music.

**Solo**—To "solo" a signal means to engage the button on the mixer that effectively mutes all other channels in the mix, leaving the soloed signal by itself for analysis. Sometimes labeled PFL (pre-fader listen) or AFL (after-fader listen), depending on where the signal is tapped off. Also refers to the button that switches this function in or out.

**Spaced Pair**—A miking arrangement where two mic's are hung over the source (such as a drumset) at a distance from each other, utilizing time differences as well as amplitude differences for stereo imaging. Also known as AB miking. (See *Coincident Pair*.)

**Splatter**—A condition where an excess of high-frequency energy (usually from cymbals) bleeds into the other mic's, making it hard to get a clean sound from the rest of the drumkit.

**Sustain**—The part of a note following the attack. This is where the fundamental pitch is, giving the note body and warmth. On a drum, the sustain can be enhanced with good tuning and proper EQ. (See *Attack*.)

**Talkback**—A feature on the mixing console that lets the engineer (in the control room) talk to the musicians (in the studio) by sending a mic' signal to the cue mix, usually via the headphone buss. Also refers to the small microphone that is built into many mixers for this purpose.

**Threshold**—The level (usually set by the user) on dynamic processors that determines the point at which the processing will begin. As examples, a signal above the threshold will cause a gate to open or a limiter to engage.

**Transient**—The short, sharp peak of a percussive waveform, usually occurring during the beginning or "attack" portion of a sound. Accurate reproduction of transients is essential in order to faithfully capture drum sounds.

**Wet**—A processed signal, especially one with reverb applied to it. (See *Dry*.)

# Other Books From Modern Drummer

## Applied Rhythms
### by Carl Palmer
Transcriptions of ten of Carl Palmer's most famous recordings.

## The Electronic Drummer
### by Norman Weinberg
From simple uses of electronics to complex setups.

## The Best Of Concepts
### by Roy Burns
Informative and entertaining ideas on dozens of subjects that concern all drummers.

## The Great American Drums
### by Harry Cangany
The history of American drum manufacturing and a valuable collector's reference source.

## The Best Of MD: Rock
Everything from linear drumming, playing in odd time signatures, and double bass techniques.

## The Great Jazz Drummers
### by Ron Spagnardi
This book tells the stories of over 60 legendary drumming greats. Sound Supplement included.

## When In Doubt, Roll
### by Bill Bruford
Transcriptions of 18 of Bruford's greatest recorded performances with commentary and exercises.

## Master Studies
### by Joe Morello
*The* book on hand development and drumstick control.

## Creative Timekeeping
### by Rick Mattingly
A challenging approach to true independence.

## The New Breed
### by Gary Chester
This book will help you develop the skills needed to master today's studio requirements.

## Drum Wisdom
### by Bob Moses
The unique and refreshing concepts of one of the most exceptional drummers of our time.

## The Cymbal Book
### by Hugo Pinksterboer
Cymbal history, acoustics, selection, cleaning, and repairing. Over 200 pages.

See your local music dealer or contact Hal Leonard Publishing Corporation at 777 W. Bluemound Road, P.O. Box 13819, Milwaukee, WI 53213.